Children and the Environment

Children and the Environment

Martin Rosenbaum

ISBN 1 874 579 01 6

Published by the National Children's Bureau
8 Wakley Street
London EC1V 7QE

Registered Charity Number 258825

Telephone 071 278 9441

Typeset, printed and bound by Saxon Printing Ltd, Derby.

Cover printed on recycled board.
Text printed on 90gsm recycled paper.

The National Children's Bureau was established as a registered charity in 1963. Our purpose is to identify and promote the interests of all children and young people and to improve their status in a diverse and multiracial society.

We work closely with professionals and policy makers to improve the lives of all children but especially children under five, those affected by family instability and children with special needs or disabilities.

We collect and disseminate information about children and promote good practice in children's services through research, policy and practice development, publications, seminars, training and an extensive library and information service.

Contents

Foreword

This unique book is an important contribution to advocacy for children who are still the least heard members of our society and whose lack of a vote ensures their need for representation.

In a well-researched and controlled exposition Martin Rosenbaum makes the facts speak for themselves through an examination of the environmental elements which we need to survive like clean air, clean water and clean land. He explores the vulnerability of children's 'small, developing and physiologically immature bodies' to the careless, selfish and shortsighted policies and behaviour of adults and governments. Some of the examples he gives will shock even readers who have long had children's interests at heart.

He provides a clear and persuasive action list, with which no one could argue. He reiterates his call for a Children's Rights Commissioner who could influence policy makers to take account of children's interests.

He concludes with a plea for children to be given more opportunity to take part directly in the policy making process and have their views taken into account.

At the National Children's Bureau we believe these issues are crucial and that is why we commissioned this book. We hope it will be read widely and act as a spur to further action.

Barbara Kahan OBE
Chair
National Children's Bureau

Preface

Many environmental problems affect the health and well-being of children much more than adults. But despite the high profile of green issues in recent years, this fact has achieved surprisingly little prominence.

When I told people I was writing a book about 'children and the environment', many – particularly those from green organisations – immediately assumed it was an explanation of environmental topics aimed at children. Some thought it was a book about what children could do to improve the environment, and a couple thought it must be about how children do it harm. Few realised without further explanation that in fact it was about how damage to our environment disproportionately hurts children.

Much has been written for children about the environment, including the role they can play in protecting it. And accounts of individual environmental dangers often make the point that children are especially at risk. But of the enormous quantity of material published in recent years about the environment, very little has looked in detail at its impact on children as a group. The few books that have done so either concentrate on a limited field (such as air pollution), are 'self-help' guides aimed at advising parents rather than analysis of policy, or adopt a global approach and therefore focus on children in poorer countries where on the whole environmental threats are much greater.

This book is an attempt to fill the gap, by identifying and examining the main environmental problems in the UK which particularly affect children and proposing priorities for change. It aims to bring a children's perspective to public debate about environmental issues, and help persuade decision takers, opinion formers and the public of the importance of the impact on children of environmental policy-making.

Naturally many people have helped me with information, ideas and comments on drafts. They include Leslie Alexander, Jack Ashley, Jane Ashley, Jon Ayres, Tony Brett Young, Derek Bryce-Smith, Patrick Candler, Ray Cartwright, Sue Cavanagh, Frances Clarke, Madeleine Cobbing, Jan Cosgrove, Jonathan Couriel, Hugo Crombie, Martyn Day, Anthony Dayan, Peter Duffin, Sarah Finch, Matthew Gaines, Malcolm Green, Patrick Green, John Hickman, Mayer Hillman, Sean Humber, Julie Jaspert, Ann Link, Anna Lubelska, Rona MacKie, Graham Maclachlan, Sue Milner, Michael Moore, Sally Moore, Peter Newell, Ray Ranson, Philippa Russell, Robin Russell Jones, Arjun Sen, Lynn Sloman, Chris Whitehouse, Martin Wright, and numerous officials, who may prefer not to be named, in the Departments of Environment, Transport and Health, the Scottish Office, the Drinking Water Inspectorate and HM Inspectorate of Pollution. I am also grateful to Fiona Blakemore, Anne Weyman and Alison Forbes of the National Children's Bureau. Responsibility for the text is of course all mine, and the views expressed are not necessarily those of the Bureau.

Martin Rosenbaum
November 1992

1. Introduction

> 'There are clear moral reasons why efforts to end environmental degradation must focus on children ... children are too often the victims of pollution – their young bodies make them far more vulnerable than adults to the poisons we spew into the air, and toxins we sow on earth. Moreover, the problem of environmental degradation is essentially a problem for children – not adults. They, and those still unborn, will inherit the earth we leave them. Their futures are in our hands – only we can protect it for them.'
> (UNICEF/UNEP, 1990, p1)

The Government defines hazardous waste in terms of the amount that would be necessary to kill or seriously injure a young child. Under the Control of Pollution (Special Waste) Regulations 1980, waste is considered 'special' – the most dangerous category – if a child weighing 20 kilos who swallowed five cubic centimetres would be likely to suffer death or serious harm. This is an official if somewhat macabre illustration of the fact that children are more vulnerable to toxic pollution than adults – one of the underlying themes of this book.

This book only deals with children in the UK. The environmental difficulties faced by children in eastern Europe, the former Soviet Union and developing countries are of course far greater. In developing countries for example contaminated drinking water is a major cause of child deaths. UNICEF estimates that each year about four million under fives die of diarrhoeal diseases, and these are mainly the result of waterborne viral and bacterial infections (UNICEF/UNEP, 1990, p25). But although the UK's environmental problems are small in comparison, they still have serious implications for the health and well-being of the country's children.

The environmental movement often appeals to the notion of 'inter-generational justice'. It emphasises frequently, and rightly so, the moral obligation to be fair to future generations which will inhabit the planet. This means we should not deplete its natural resources at an unsustainable rate, leave 'pollution time-bombs' that will wreak their damage a long time hence, or otherwise build up an excessive burden of environmental degradation to be sorted out at a later date.

This is fine as far as it goes, but there is a more immediate notion of inter-generational justice – the need to be fair to all present generations. This demands that since children are particularly vulnerable to environmental harm, we take special steps to protect them. Some of these steps are outlined in this book.

It is often argued that children tend to be particularly enthusiastic supporters of environmental causes. For example, Lloyd Timberlake and Laura Thomas put it as follows:

Children care deeply about the environment. British company directors surveyed in 1989 said the main reason for their own growing concern for the environment was the regular haranguing they were getting from their children on the state of the world. Opinion polls, the stacks of new books telling children how to be green and the sacks of mail from schoolchildren to environmental groups all reflect this youthful concern for the state of the world (Timberlake and Thomas, 1990, p58).

Children are playing their part in protecting the environment. Let us ensure that at the same time we strive for an environment which properly protects children.

2. Children's vulnerability

'Waste is to be regarded as dangerous to life for the purposes of these regulations if – (a) a single dose of not more than five cubic centimetres would be likely to cause death or serious damage to tissue if ingested by a child of 20 kilograms body weight ... '
Control of Pollution (Special Waste) Regulations 1980

Children tend to be particularly affected by environmental problems for three main reasons: their physiology, their behaviour and their status in society.

Physiology

Children tend to be more susceptible to the health effects of pollution because they are small, growing and biologically less prepared for many of life's hazards. Generally the younger the child, the more this is true. (The child in the womb is usually even more vulnerable, at least to substances which cross the placenta).

Because children are small, a particular quantity of a particular pollutant will affect them more than an adult. Furthermore, in proportion to their body weight, children inhale more air and drink more water than adults (Plunkett, Turnbull and Rodricks, 1992, pp 79-82; World Health Organisation (WHO), 1986, pp 16, 22). This makes them more vulnerable to the ill effects of polluted air and water. Some chemicals can also be absorbed through the skin. Children are again more vulnerable because they have a larger surface area in proportion to their body weight and compounds absorbed through a given part of the skin will result in higher body tissue concentrations than in adults (WHO, 1986, pp 15, 24/5).

Their size affects them in other ways too. For example, since the airways in their lungs are narrower in the first place, children suffer more breathing difficulties if inhaling polluted air leads to constriction (narrowing) of the airways. And when indoors young children can be more vulnerable to the harmful effects of gases which concentrate near the floor, such as certain pesticides (Fenske, 1992).

Furthermore the gastro-intestinal tract tends to be more permeable in children, so that compared to adults they frequently absorb into their bodies larger quantities of pollutants which they have ingested. This is particularly true of heavy metals such as lead and various radioactive elements. Enhanced absorption seems to continue until puberty. It has also been argued that the lungs and the skin are more absorbent in children (Plunkett, Turnbull and Rodricks, 1992, pp 84-6).

Once children have absorbed a dangerous substance, their immature body systems may process it differently from the way that adults would. The main role in detoxifying the body is played by the kidneys, liver and enzyme system. In young children these are often less efficient at neutralising toxicants and eliminating them from the body (Plunkett, Turnbull and Rodricks, 1992, pp 86-91). In particular, children's bodies generally take longer to eliminate organic chemicals (WHO, 1986, pp 37, 39). (However there are some substances, such as certain drugs, which young children eliminate more efficiently than adults).

Some toxic chemicals are stored in body fat. Because children on the whole have less body fat, these fat-soluble chemicals circulate in the blood throughout the body for a longer period instead of being stored (UNICEF/UNEP, 1990, p24).

Their immune system is also less able to combat disease. Immunity to a disease is built up through an occurrence of that disease, so children tend to have less immunity and are more likely for example to develop gastro-enteritis from contact with particular bacteria, such as those from sewage-contaminated beaches. The consequences of disease can also be greater for children. For example in the case of diarrhoea, babies tend to become dehydrated more quickly due to their greater fluid requirement for their weight.

The other factor which makes children more vulnerable to pollution is because they are developing. This means that toxicants which affect or impede development can have permanent consequences. For example, the damaging impact of lead on a child's brain may reduce intellectual capacity throughout life. Air pollution can also have long-term effects. Respiratory disease in childhood can lead to lifelong difficulties.

In 1991 the British Medical Association (BMA) identified children as a 'high-risk sub-section of the population, ... who experience toxic effects at lower levels of exposure than the general population ... and may require special protective measures'. The BMA stated:

'Foetuses, neonates, infants and children are recognised to be vulnerable to the toxic effects of hazardous substances. This is because of the immaturity of their body systems, the possibility that a single exposure might lead to a permanent defect and to immaturity of protective detoxification mechanisms' (BMA, 1991, pp 87-8).

Behaviour

Children's normal behaviour can increase their exposure to certain environmental hazards in a number of ways.

They tend to spend more time in vigorous exercise outdoors than adults, so they breathe more air pollution into their lungs. Children who play in the street will encounter more car fumes and dust containing lead.

Children are sometimes more at risk because they are less aware of the dangers of particular activities. Playing on derelict industrial or waste disposal sites can bring exposure to polluted areas. Playing on the ground outdoors can also bring them closer to health risks, such as from dog excrement. Young children are likely to place in their mouths fingers, soil or objects which may carry dirt or dust contaminated with pollutants.

Status

Children are a large sector of the population, but uniquely lacking in power. They play no part in the political process which determines nationally and locally the policies that affect their lives. As a result the impact of policy on children receives insufficient care and attention.

In the context of this book this is particularly important in relation to the chapters on transport and the built environment.

These illustrate practical consequences of the treatment of children as a low political priority whose viewpoint and rights are often ignored. As Mayer Hillman of the Policy Studies Institute and colleagues say about the way children's independent freedom of movement has been reduced by road traffic, children have lost out 'without society apparently noticing' (Hillman, Adams and Whitelegg, 1990, p95).

Not surprisingly children from social groups with least influence usually face the biggest problems. For example, highly polluting industrial plants are usually located amidst poor communities, and children from lower social classes are much more likely to be killed or seriously injured in road accidents. Similarly the built environment is even more inconvenient for children with disabilities.

3. Drinking water

'He who drinks a tumbler of London water has literally in his stomach more animated beings than there are men, women and children on the face of the globe.'
Sydney Smith (1771-1845)

The water from our taps inevitably contains small quantities of all sorts of substances. Water is a powerful solvent which collects many impurities on its journey to the home through rivers, groundwater, reservoirs, treatment works (where some substances are removed and others added) and pipes. It is also excellent at supporting minute forms of life. Some of these impurities do not matter significantly to the health of the drinkers, but others may do.

The law recognises that the suitability of British drinking water can be adversely affected by a wide variety of contaminants. The Water Supply (Water Quality) Regulations 1989, which incorporate requirements from the European Community drinking water directive (EC, 1980a), cover 57 parameters of water quality, ranging from toxic chemicals to microbiological organisms. Even this does not deal with all contaminants that can harm the health of water drinkers. For example, they do not refer to cryptosporidium, a waterborne parasite responsible for a number of recent localised outbreaks of illness and diarrhoea.

Children are more vulnerable to contaminated water. Infants and young children have a higher intake of water for their weight than older children, who in turn have a higher intake than adults. Therefore 'infants and children ... receive a higher dose of a water contaminant than would an adult using the same source of water' (Plunkett, Turnbull and Rodricks, p82). However their comparatively immature body systems are less able to deal with chemical and biological pollutants (see pp 3-5 on the greater vulnerability of children generally to pollution).

Lead

The most prominent campaign over the past few years involving children's health and the environment was against use of lead in petrol. This is now declining dramatically (see pp 26-7) with beneficial effects on lead levels in the air and children's bodies. However concern still exists about the threat to children posed by lead in drinking water.

Lead is a poison, a neurotoxin which damages the nervous system. The consequences of acute lead poisoning include nerve and brain damage, stomach pains, anaemia, comas and ultimately death. However, acute poisoning is rare these days. Concern instead has focused on the cumulative impact of long-term exposure to low levels of lead in the environment, particularly on the relationship between this and children's intelligence. Lead has been put to many more industrial and commercial applications than other toxic metals, and this has resulted in substantial quantities finding their way into the environment and human bodies. One major use was in domestic plumbing systems and the water distribution network.

Children are especially vulnerable because their brains and nervous systems are still developing. Lead impedes the development of interneuronal connections in the brain which happens most rapidly in the early years of life. Children also absorb ingested lead more quickly and easily than adults. A given increase in lead concentrations in drinking water results in an increase in children's blood lead levels three or four times greater than adults' (Davis and Grant, 1992, p154). The impact is also greater in very young children because their blood-brain barrier is not completely developed. Furthermore some children take in lead through dust on objects they chew or suck.

Several studies from different countries linking children's body lead levels with reduced intelligence made news in the 1970s. Originally the subject of much scientific controversy, the connection has been examined extensively and is now widely accepted.

In 1982 Sir Henry Yellowlees, then the Government's Chief Medical Officer, stated: 'Even at low blood levels there is a negative correlation between blood lead levels and IQ of which the simplest explanation is that the lead produces these effects' (Wilson, 1983, p30).

Probably the most influential study was that of over 2,000 schoolchildren in Massachusetts, USA carried out in the late 1970s (Needleman et al, 1979). This found that the higher the lead level in children's teeth (an indicator of body lead levels), the more likely they were to have low IQ scores and to be thought by their teachers to exhibit certain characteristics of poor behaviour including distractibility, impulsiveness and inability to follow directions.

A more recent major British study (Fulton et al, 1987) of 500 Edinburgh children aged six to nine found that those with higher blood lead levels performed less well on intellectual, numeracy and reading tests. After taking into account social factors which would affect the children's performance, this found that the difference between the ten per cent of children with the highest lead levels and the ten per cent with the lowest averaged six points on the British IQ scale. Since performance was impaired even in children with average lead levels, the results suggest that most children in British cities have absorbed enough lead to hinder their intellectual development. The authors conclude that there is 'no evidence of a safe level' of exposure to lead.

A wide variety of other studies have linked lead to learning difficulties and behavioural problems in children, including im-paired manual and visual coordination, inability to concentrate, hyperactivity and aggression.

One study referred specifically to lead in tap water. Carried out in the seventies at Glasgow University, this found that 'water-lead concentrations in the maternal home during pregnancy correlated with blood-lead concentrations in mentally retarded children'. Babies born to mothers who drank water with a high lead content were twice as likely to be 'mentally retarded' (Moore, Meredith and Goldberg, 1977).

Lead enters drinking water primarily through lead plumbing, which features in millions of British households, mainly those built before 1945 but including some built until the mid-70s. It is estimated very roughly that 9.4 million properties in England and Wales have internal lead plumbing or lead pipes connecting them to the mains, about 45 per cent of the total. About one in 13 of these lead piped properties are non-domestic, which would include schools and hospitals as well as offices and factories (Water Research Centre, 1992, pp 21, 54). Some contamination also results from lead in older parts of the water distribution network, and lead solder used to join copper pipes in modern plumbing systems.

The presence of lead in pipework causes the biggest problems in areas with soft water, since this is more acidic and dissolves lead (and other metals) much more easily. These include parts of the Midlands, much of the South West, most of Merseyside, and most of Scotland and Northern Ireland. But some significant pollution also occurs in certain hard water areas. Other factors which influence lead concentration include the age of the plumbing, vibration of the pipes, the temperature of the water and the time for which it is left standing.

Tap water is a major source of lead intake for large numbers of British children. Bottle-fed babies are particularly at risk (Davis and Grant, 1992, p152). Significantly higher lead levels have been found in people who live in areas with 'plumbosolvent' (lead dissolving) tapwater and also those who live in homes built before 1945 (Hunter, 1986, p105). Residents in plumbosolvent areas may get 50 per cent of the lead in their bodies from water (Russell Jones, 1989). As leaded petrol becomes less common, lead in tapwater will become relatively more important.

The maximum lead concentration in tap water allowed by the Government's water quality regulations is 50 µg/l (micrograms per litre). In 1991 this was exceeded at domestic sampling points in 26 per cent of the 2,577 water supply zones in England and Wales created for the purpose of monitoring water quality (Drinking Water Inspectorate (DWI), 1992a, p248). Because lead contamination is strongly influenced by the pipework in individual houses, this does not imply that every household in these zones has water above the limit. Equally it does not imply that in the other zones no household's water is breaking the limit. But what the figures do indicate is the widespread extent of the problem.

In some areas the situation is much worse. For example the limit was exceeded in 72 per cent of the zones in the area served by North West Water, which supplies nearly seven million people (DWI, 1992a, p135).

Official figures have only been published by the newly created Drinking Water Inspectorate since 1991. They follow numerous surveys in the 1970s and 1980s which found many locations with very high lead concentrations, especially in Scotland. And more recently a joint Friends of the Earth/*Observer* survey in 1989 found several places where concentrations were many times greater than the current UK limit of 50 μg/l (see Children's Legal Centre, 1989, and Rose, 1990, p98).

However not only is the UK limit frequently exceeded, there is also much evidence to suggest that in any case it is too lenient. In 1989 an official Ministry of Agriculture, Fisheries and Food (MAFF) working party recommended that adults should not be exposed to average lead concentrations in drinking water above 30 μg/l, and for bottle-fed babies this figure should be 10-15 μg/l (MAFF, 1989, p18). At time of writing it seems highly likely that the World Health Organisation will soon recommend a limit significantly lower than the UK's, probably 10 μg/l. It is expected that in due course the EC directive would then be revised to incorporate this new lower figure.

The consensus of the scientific evidence is that even very low levels of lead impair children's intelligence, and that the presence of lead in tapwater at current concentrations is damaging the mental abilities of many children in the UK. Although other aspects of drinking water pollution such as nitrates and pesticides have attracted more publicity, it is lead which presents the most important health problem.

The way to eliminate the lead is to get rid of lead piping. The problem is that to do this comprehensively would be extremely expensive. Research carried out in 1991/92 for the Department of the Environment estimated the cost of replacing all lead plumbing in England and Wales at £8.2 billion (Water Research Centre, 1992, pp 32-3).

The situation is complicated by the fact that although it is the responsibility of water companies to supply non-plumbosolvent water, it is up to individual householders to replace their own pipes. At a cost of hundreds of pounds many cannot afford to do so, and the availability of local authority housing renovation grants is severely restricted. An Institution of Environmental Health Officers (IEHO) survey of 300 councils in England and Wales (74 per cent of those with relevant responsibilities) found that in

1990/91 between them they had made just 1,450 grants for work which included replacing lead piping (IEHO, 1992).

This is despite the Royal Commission on Environmental Pollution which stated in 1983 (RCEP, 1983, p141):

> The criteria for the award of home improvement or repair grants for the replacement of lead plumbing should be reviewed, with the aim of making such grants more widely available. Publicity campaigns should be conducted in areas where pipe replacement is considered necessary ... Financial constraints should not be allowed to hamper the pipe replacement programme.

Measures other than pipe replacement can help but will not completely solve the problem. Lead intake can be significantly reduced by always running some water off whenever it has been left standing for some time, for example first thing in the morning. However, although this is a sensible procedure for health reasons, it wastes water and furthermore the introduction of water metering is likely to deter people from doing so.

To reduce plumbosolvency, water companies add chemicals such as calcium carbonate (lime) or orthophosphate to their supplies. This has helped considerably, especially in Scotland and East Anglia, but there is a limit to which this can reduce lead levels. Altering plumbosolvency is unlikely to guarantee satisfying a lower requirement of the sort which the World Health Organisation will soon recommend. Assuming the EC adopts a revised WHO guideline, then in due course the Government will have little alternative except to set in motion a major programme of replacing lead plumbing.

Nitrates

Nitrate pollution of drinking water has been the subject of much publicity in recent years due to widespread breaches of the EC limit and the government's long-running battle over this with environmental pressure groups. The problem stems mainly from agricultural use of nitrogen-based fertilisers which has increased dramatically since the 1950s. The extensive ploughing up of pasture land which soaked up nitrates is also to blame. As a result nitrates slowly leach from the land into rivers, reservoirs and groundwater, and then into tap water which is drawn from these sources. It can take years, sometimes perhaps even decades, to reach some underground water supplies, and it seems likely that future problems have therefore already been set in train (see for example London Food Commission, 1988, pp 124-5).

In 1991, four per cent of water supply zones in England and Wales were found to have exceeded the EC and UK regulatory limit of 50 mg/l (milligrams per litre). These zones were concentrated in East Anglia and neighbouring counties – 16 per cent of the zones covered by Anglian Water failed to comply with the limit (Drinking Water Inspectorate, 1992a, pp 248, 28). Previous studies have shown East Anglia and the Midlands to be the regions worst affected by nitrate pollution.

Nitrate causes concern because it is known that it can lead to methaemoglobinaemia, a potentially fatal disease in babies. Bacteria in the human mouth and digestive system convert nitrates into nitrites, which can react with blood in a way which reduces its capacity to carry oxygen. This is methaemoglobinaemia, commonly called 'blue baby syndrome' due to the blue skin colour resulting from lack of blood oxygen. It is not a major risk for adults but can be very serious for small babies, especially those under three months. They are more susceptible because their blood is affected more easily and their enzyme reduction system is insufficiently developed to restore their blood's oxygen-carrying capacity. They also produce less acid in their stomachs and this leaves them with more bacteria which make nitrates into nitrites (Dudley, 1986, p30).

However, methaemoglobinaemia is not currently a serious problem in the UK. According to the Government's Chief Medical Officer, there were only 14 reported cases in the period 1950-1985. The last case was in 1972 and the last death in 1950 (Dudley, 1986, p67). On the other hand it has been argued that babies may suffer from nitrate-induced oxygen deficiency without showing the clinical symptoms that would lead to a report of the disease (Timberlake and Thomas, 1990, p97; Mansfield and Monro, 1987, p31).

The Chief Medical Officer's advice is that where levels are above 50 mg/l, health authorities should monitor for methaemoglobinaemia and where they are above 100 mg/l alternative water supplies should be provided for infant feeding. The health threat has been taken sufficiently seriously that in some high-nitrate areas arrangements have been made to supply separate water to babies. In 1987 villages near Ripon in Yorkshire had bottled water provided for babies under six months because of the high nitrate level in the local supply (*Environment Digest*, November 1987). Similar action was taken in Hull in 1988 (McConville, 1990, p145). In East Anglia some babies have been prescribed bottled water, and Anglian Water has had two mobile bottling plants ready to supply infants with low-nitrate water in case this is required (London Food Commission, 1988, p111). The water company states (personal communication) that its contingency plans involving bottling facilities are in case of any excessive contamination, but nitrates seem to be the most likely cause.

It has also been argued that nitrates are linked to stomach cancer but this is disputed, and the research evidence appears to be inconclusive (British Medical Association, 1992a, p49).

The Government and the water companies have pledged that all the UK's water supplies will comply with the EC limit by 1995. This will be accomplished mainly through expensive steps of blending with low-nitrate supplies or installing denitrification treatment processes. The Government is also taking steps to reduce nitrogen fertiliser use in the worst hit areas.

Although the current health effects of nitrate pollution appear to be limited, it is important to keep nitrates well under control. This need is reinforced given that levels in some groundwater sources will probably continue to rise for several years if not longer due to past fertiliser use.

Bacterial contamination

In 1991 seven per cent of the water supply zones in England and Wales were found to have exceeded the regulatory limit for coliform bacteria. Although these are not necessarily harmful in themselves, their presence is usually taken to indicate the possible presence of other disease-causing bacteria. Eleven per cent of zones exceeded the limit for faecal coliforms, which usually indicate contamination by sewage or farm slurry. (Sometimes however taps or pipework in a household may themselves become contaminated, perhaps due to poor hygiene). Thames Water, which supplies over 7 million people, was one of the worst areas. The faecal coliform limit was broken in 32 per cent of the company's water supply zones (DWI, 1992a, pp 248,206).

It is impossible to say what effect such bacterial pollution has had. However children are more likely to be vulnerable to any health effects, which would most probably involve gastro-enteritis, diarrhoea, and other gastro-intestinal symptoms.

Cryptosporidium

Cryptosporidium is a parasitic micro-organism which can cause stomach pain and diarrhoea. It is more likely to be a significant threat to health in the case of young children. The organism lives in the guts of farm animals and enters water supplies via farm slurry. It is not clear how prevalent it is in British tapwater, since it is difficult to detect and measure.

It is only recently that cryptosporidium-contaminated tapwater has been identified as a cause of diarrhoea and illness, but in the past few years several such outbreaks have been blamed on it. The disease of cryptosporidiosis can affect people of any age but is most common in children aged one to five (British Medical Association, 1992a, p49). For example in February 1989 over 100 cases were recorded of children in Oxfordshire and Swindon suffering vomiting and diarrhoea as a result of contact with the organism. The public was told to boil all water intended for children under two. Other outbreaks have occurred in Hull, Sheffield, Surrey and Ayrshire (Friends of the Earth, 1990). (Infection with the organism can also be due to contact with infected animals and the water supply is therefore not always to blame). The water industry is researching ways to detect and eliminate the organism.

Other pollutants

Health concerns have also been raised about a wide variety of other pollutants which may be present in tapwater in small quantities. These include pesticides (particularly atrazine and simazine); chlorinated solvents used in cleaning processes; trihalomethanes such as chloroform which are by-products of disinfection processes involving chlorine; polycyclic aromatic hydrocarbons which are carcinogenic and may leach from old pipes lined with coal tar pitch;

seepage pollution from old toxic waste landfill sites; and toxins released into rivers and reservoirs by blue-green algae.

In the case of certain pesticides there are frequent examples of local water supplies exceeding the EC limits which are also embodied in the UK's regulations (see Drinking Water Inspectorate, 1992a and 1992b). The water industry argues that these limits are not based on health grounds and the quantities in tap water therefore constitute no danger. Nevertheless due to the EC directive it is installing means of treatment to reduce pesticide levels over the next few years. The cumulative effects of long-term low level exposure to many pesticides are a matter of controversy and this issue has been vigorously pursued by organisations such as Parents for Safe Food, the Food Commission and Friends of the Earth. However intake from pesticide residues in food is much more important than that due to drinking water, and the impact of food on children's health falls outside the remit of this book.

Generally there is clear evidence that most of the substances listed above as other potential pollutants are harmful if consumed in sufficient quantities. As usual children would be particularly vulnerable. At this stage it is impossible to identify any specific damage to children's health which has been caused by the presence of any of these substances in tapwater. However it is prudent if nothing else to control their concentrations.

Recommendations

The Government should institute a publicly-funded rolling programme of removing lead pipes entirely from the mains water distribution system and from homes, schools, hospitals and other buildings. The cost of such a programme means that it would have to take several years, but it should start in the worst affected areas and for the whole operation a ten-year time span would be realistic.

Until this happens:

- The Department of Health, the Health Education Authority, and (in the affected areas) health authorities and local authority environmental health departments should give greater publicity to the hazard posed by lead piping, the advantages of replacing it and the ways in which the risk can be minimised while it is still in place.
- Local authorities should give greater priority to housing renovation grants for the replacement of lead plumbing.
- Householders with children should arrange for their own lead pipes to be replaced, or if this is not possible, should reduce the risk by adopting a habit of running off water which has been standing.
- Water companies should reinforce their efforts to reduce plumbosolvency and extend the grants some already give to householders for lead pipe replacement.

Water companies should also reinforce their efforts to tackle contamination by bacteria and other micro-organisms.

4. Air pollution

'... the effects of pollution by motor vehicles can be summarised as follows. There is no evidence that this type of air pollution has any adverse effect on health.'
Ministry of Transport paper to Clean Air Council, 1970 (quoted in Holman and Festing, 1991, p3)

'We are very, very concerned that transport can destroy and damage people's health and we want to eliminate that as far as we can.'
Cecil Parkinson, then Secretary of State for Transport, 10 November 1989 (quoted in Adams, 1990, p7)

Ever since our ancestors set fire to wood to warm their caves, humans have been polluting the air and damaging their lungs as a result. Today however we go about it in a much bigger way. In immense quantities we burn coal to generate electricity, we ignite petrol to power motor vehicles, we burn toxic waste to try to get rid of it, and we operate all sorts of industrial processes that contaminate the air we breathe.

The results of such human activity were illustrated by the smog affecting several major British cities in December 1991, which caused the highest recorded atmospheric levels of the important pollutant, nitrogen dioxide. However, Britain's most notorious air pollution episode was the London smog of December 1952, believed to have killed around 4,000 people. Most of the victims were elderly and in poor health, but children under one were also badly affected – the death rate among under ones doubled (UNICEF/UNEP, 1990, p28). Earlier smogs undoubtedly also caused many deaths, but this one aroused an unprecedented level of media and public outrage which forced government action. The

1956 Clean Air Act controlled domestic and industrial smoke output, paved the way for local authorities to create 'smokeless zones', and provided for grants for households to convert to smokeless fuels.

As a result not only of these measures but also of changes in the general pattern of domestic and industrial fuel use, smoke and sulphur dioxide pollution declined dramatically. This created a widespread feeling of complacency that air pollution was no longer a problem in Britain. The Clean Air Council was abolished in 1979, and the Air Pollution Unit of the Medical Research Council in 1980. Since then there has been a dearth of UK research into the health effects of air pollution, although very recently there has been a renewal of interest. The current need for more research funding has been stressed by the Department of Health's own advisers (Advisory Group on the Medical Aspects of Air Pollution Episodes, 1991).

But in fact while some pollutants have been diminishing, others have risen, especially those produced by road traffic, which are less visible and therefore less obvious than smoke. While industry and power stations are still major sources of air pollution, the car has replaced coal-burning as the most important cause of all.

Modern air can contain a wide variety of pollutants. Some are produced in large quantities across the country, others come from particular local industrial sites. The problem naturally tends to be much worse in urban areas, but pollutants can travel large distances, especially when emitted from tall chimneys. This chapter looks mainly at pollutants which are widespread across Britain, but also at some more localised problems.

Air pollution harms human health mainly by causing or aggravating respiratory problems and diseases. However it is also a route by which people can take in toxicants (such as lead) which damage other parts of the body. On the whole it affects children more seriously than it affects adults because:

- compared to their body weight children inhale more air, and therefore air pollution, than adults do. At rest a child under three inhales twice as much air per unit of body weight as an adult (UNICEF/UNEP, 1990, p28; see also Plunkett, Turnbull and Rodricks, pp 79-80);
- the airways in their lungs are narrower. Any constriction due to

irritation by air pollution is therefore more likely to result in airways which are so narrow as to cause breathing problems;

- since their lungs are still maturing, long-term effects are likely to be worse. Exposure to pollution could have a permanent impact on the way a child's lungs develop. Contracting respiratory disease in childhood can lead to lifelong difficulties (Roberts, 1992, p11);

- vigorous exercise increases air intake and therefore pollution intake. Children tend to spend more time exercising outside and are therefore likely to receive higher doses of pollution;

- it has also been argued that children tend to breathe more through their mouths. As a result matter which would otherwise be trapped in the nasal passages reaches the lungs where it can injure lung tissue or be absorbed into the bloodstream (Green, 1991, p34).

It is often difficult to link cause and effect in the field of air pollution. Pollutants often occur together so that isolating the damaging ones is not easy. It can also be problematic to eliminate confounding factors, notably smoking and passive smoking. Nevertheless if we look at the levels and potential health effects of the UK's main air pollutants in the light of international research we find substantial cause for concern for children's health.

Nitrogen oxides

Nitrogen oxides (compounds of nitrogen and oxygen) are an important cause of acid rain and consequent damage to waterborne life, vegetation and buildings, and can also be harmful to human health. They are produced as a result of combustion processes in which nitrogen in the air and fuel reacts with oxygen. This mainly creates nitric oxide at first but in the atmosphere it rapidly converts to nitrogen dioxide, the most important oxide of nitrogen in terms of air pollution.

It is estimated (Department of the Environment (DoE), 1992a, p8) that in 1990 the UK produced 2.7 million tonnes of nitrogen oxides, of which 51 per cent came from road transport and 28 per cent from power stations. Nitrogen oxide emissions are rising steadily. The 1990 figure is an 18 per cent increase on the 1980 total. The growth is entirely accounted for by road transport emissions which increased by 72 per cent in this period, while power station and industrial emissions slightly fell.

Urban areas throughout the world have significant levels of nitrogen dioxide and Britain is no exception. The European Community directive on nitrogen dioxide (EC, 1985) contains a limit value which should not be exceeded for immediate health reasons and guide values which are aimed at longer term protection. A monitoring site in the Cromwell Road, central London, has consistently recorded levels above or very close to the EC limit (DoE, 1992a, pp 9-10). The less stringent guide values were exceeded in 1990 at five sites – four in London and one in Manchester – out of the UK's 12 permanent automatic monitoring sites. Four of these – three in London – also breached the guidelines of the World Health Organisation (WHO) (Broughton et al, 1992, p52). The WHO guidelines are drawn up on a different basis from the EC ones and are not directly comparable in terms of stringency, but they are also aimed at protecting health.

The annual statistics for the 12 permanent sites for 1991 have not been published at time of writing, but due to the December 1991 smog the London figures will include the highest nitrogen dioxide levels since records began, more than double the WHO guidelines (Warren Spring Laboratory, 1992).

A much wider official survey, involving less sophisticated and cheaper temporary measuring devices, found that the EC guide values were exceeded in 1991 in large parts of the UK, covering approximately a third of the population. In this survey the worst affected places were Sheffield, London and Manchester. On the previous occasion this exercise was conducted in 1986, only eight per cent of the sites had exceeded the guide values, compared to 33 per cent in 1991 *(The Independent*, 15 and 16 May 1992).

Nitrogen dioxide is damaging to health. The Department of the Environment states (DoE, 1992a, p8) that 'acute exposure [to nitrogen dioxide] can cause transient respiratory problems and reduce lung function'. According to Friends of the Earth (Holman and Festing, 1991, p18), 'Nitrogen dioxide can increase susceptibility to viral infection, irritate the lungs and cause bronchitis and pneumonia. Research has shown that acute exposure to nitrogen dioxide can cause bronchoconstriction [narrowing of the bronchial tubes in the lungs] and airway hyperactivity in asthmatics'.

Studies in the USA (Love, Lan and Shy, 1982) and Switzerland

(Rutishauser et al, 1990) have linked nitrogen dioxide to the incidence of respiratory illnesses among children. See also the new Birmingham study referred to below (p 32) for an association with asthma, and also with hospital admissions for acute respiratory disease.

Ground-level ozone

Ozone in the air can be either good or bad for our health, depending on where in the atmosphere it is. The ozone layer in the stratosphere miles above our heads is necessary because it protects the world from the sun's ultra-violet radiation, and danger arises when there is less of it – see the next chapter. However ozone in the troposphere, the lowest part of the atmosphere, is harmful because direct contact with the gas can be damaging to health.

Although some ground-level or tropospheric ozone is naturally occurring, most is formed by sunlight-aided reactions in the air between nitrogen oxides and hydrocarbons. As noted above, nitrogen oxides are issued predominantly from motor vehicle exhausts and power stations. The hydrocarbons are present in air mainly due to oil refining, petrol and solvent evaporation, and various industrial processes, as well as road traffic (DoE, 1992a, pp 10-11).

Ozone concentrations rise particularly during long hours of bright sunlight on warm, still days, and are therefore higher in the summer. Once formed the gas may persist for several days and can drift for long distances, so that rural areas can also be badly affected. High ozone episodes in the UK can be initiated in continental Europe.

None of the existing air quality directives from the European Community cover ground-level ozone, although one has been proposed by the Commission (European Commission, 1992). Guidelines aimed at protecting health have been produced by WHO. In the year April 1990 to March 1991, these guidelines were exceeded on at least several days at every one of the 18 sites in the UK's national ozone monitoring network. The worst affected site was Lullington Heath in Sussex, where the highest hour-by-hour average figure was over twice the WHO guideline and the guideline for an average reading over eight hours was breached on 53 days, a large part of the summer (Broughton et al, 1992, pp 12-48).

Ozone pollution was generally worse in the southern half of the country, a pattern which has also occurred in previous years.

According to the Department of the Environment (DoE, 1992a, pp17-18), 'High levels of ozone increase susceptibility to infections and respiratory disease and irritate the eyes, nose, throat and respiratory system'. In more detail Friends of the Earth state (Holman and Festing, 1991, p15):

At high concentrations ozone can cause severe damage to lung tissues and impair defences against bacteria and viruses. At lower concentrations ozone and other photochemical oxidants irritate the mucous membrane of the respiratory system, causing coughing, choking and impaired lung function, particularly in people who exercise. Ozone and oxidants aggravate chronic respiratory diseases such as asthma and bronchitis. These chemicals reduce resistance to respiratory infections, increasing the incidence of colds and serious diseases such as pneumonia.

In April 1992 Professor Stephen Holgate, Chairman of the Department of Health's Committee on the Medical Aspects of Air Pollution, stated that ground-level ozone could be a cause of increased asthma in babies and young children. He argued that there was growing evidence that ozone attacks babies' bronchial tubes, making them more likely to develop allergies. Prof Holgate said:

Vehicle pollution has increased dramatically in Europe, and there is now evidence that chemicals at the levels we were exposed to last summer can cause problems in the bronchial tubes. Babies appear to be particularly susceptible (unpublished paper given at National Society for Clean Air meeting, reported in *The Observer*, 12 April 1992).

Several studies in the United States (see Spektor et al, 1988) have linked increasing levels of ozone to impaired lung function amongst children, affecting their ability to take deep breaths, even though in some cases the ozone levels did not exceed WHO guidelines.

Other studies have also linked ozone levels to the frequency and severity of asthma attacks in eight to 15-year-olds and to numbers of children admitted to hospital for asthma (Read, 1991, pp 36-7).

Sulphur dioxide

Sulphur dioxide is produced by the combustion of sulphur-containing fossil fuels such as coal and oil. It is estimated (DoE, 1992a, p3) that in 1990 power stations were responsible for 72 per cent of the UK's total emissions of 3.8 million tonnes. Other industrial sources were responsible for a further 19 per cent. Emissions of sulphur dioxide are significantly less than they were 20-30 years ago, due to reduced domestic and industrial coal combustion (Mellanby, 1992, p72).

Since sulphur dioxide is often present together with smoke (small airborne particles), because they are generally produced by the same processes, their effects are often considered together. The limits for sulphur dioxide laid down in the relevant EC directive (EC, 1980b) are dependent on how much smoke is also present. The more smoke, the less sulphur dioxide is permitted.

In 1990/91 the directive limits were exceeded at three monitoring sites in Belfast. Several towns in mining areas in the north of England where coal is still widely used for domestic heating (for example Barnsley and Mansfield) are also consistently close to the limit (DoE, 1992a, pp 5-7). These places have derogations from the directive (permission not to comply) until April 1993.

There are also health-based WHO guidelines on sulphur dioxide levels which are calculated on a different basis from the EC ones. Levels in London regularly exceed these guidelines, and it seems likely that they are widely exceeded throughout Britain (Holman and Festing, 1991, pp 38-9). From April 1990 to March 1991 they were breached at seven of the country's ten automatic monitoring sites. These were in London, Belfast and the north of England.

London is one of the worst of the world's major cities for sulphur dioxide pollution (Simpson, 1990, p65). This is probably due to the number of large power stations in and around London, none of which has flue gas desulphurisation equipment fitted.

Like nitrogen dioxide, sulphur dioxide is a major cause of acid rain but also has serious implications for human health. According to the Department of the Environment (DoE, 1992a, p3), 'Sulphur dioxide can give rise to temporary respiratory problems in sensitive groups as a result of acute exposure and to an increased prevalence of respiratory problems from long-term exposure'.

Studies in North America and Europe have shown impairment of lung function in school-age children during episodes of sulphur dioxide and smoke pollution, at sulphur dioxide levels comparable to those found in some British cities (Read, 1991, pp 21-2;

UNICEF/UNEP, 1990, p28). Other research in six eastern US cities found a strong association between frequency of chronic cough, bronchitis and lower respiratory illness in pre-adolescent schoolchildren, and levels of sulphur dioxide and smoke (Ware et al, 1986). A study in Finland also found a significant association between sulphur dioxide levels and absenteeism from schools and day care centres (Pönkä, 1990).

Studies in France (Charpin et al, 1988), USA (Mostardi et al, 1981) and Israel (Goren and Hellmann, 1988) have also linked sulphur dioxide concentrations to the frequency of childhood asthma.

Health effects can also arise from the creation of 'acid aerosols'. Chemical reactions with water vapour or other gases in the atmosphere can lead to sulphur dioxide being transformed into airborne particles (aerosols) of sulphuric acid. These can penetrate the lungs, taking toxic metals and gases with them. Some scientists argue that sulphuric acid formed in this way was responsible for most of the deaths in the 1952 London smog.

Levels of acid aerosols are difficult to measure for technical reasons, but the Six Cities Study in the USA has associated them with the presence of bronchitis in ten to 12-year-olds (Read, 1991, p25).

Black smoke

This term is used to refer to the small airborne particles (often called suspended particulates) which arise from incomplete combustion of fossil fuels. In the UK their concentration is officially measured in terms of their soiling capacity and they are therefore called 'black smoke'. Until recently their main source was coal combustion, so their presence was generally associated with sulphur dioxide, but now emissions from diesel engines are increasingly responsible for black smoke. These produce much more smoke than petrol-driven engines, especially when they are badly maintained. It is estimated (DoE, 1992a, p4) that in 1990, 42 per cent of black smoke came from diesel fuel and 37 per cent from coal. As noted already, smoke concentrations have fallen dramatically over the past three decades due to clean air legislation and reduced coal consumption, although some towns in northern mining areas still have high levels.

The Department of the Environment describes the health effects of smoke as 'similar' to those of sulphur dioxide (DoE, 1992a, p3). However it is also argued that the particles carry carcinogenic hydrocarbons into the lungs (Read and Green, 1990).

Carbon monoxide

Carbon monoxide is derived from the incomplete combustion of any carbon-containing substance, including petrol. It is highly dangerous because it displaces oxygen from the blood. High concentrations can kill, while lower levels cause headaches, drowsiness, slowing down of reflexes and impaired perception. It is estimated (DoE, 1992a, p12) that in 1990 road traffic was responsible for 90 per cent of UK carbon monoxide emissions of 6.7 million tonnes. Total carbon monoxide emissions have increased by 32 per cent since 1980. This is more than accounted for by the 46 per cent increase in road traffic emissions, while other sources have dropped.

There is no EC directive regulating carbon monoxide levels. The health-based WHO guidelines were exceeded at London and Glasgow monitoring sites in the 1990/91 winter (Broughton et al, 1992, pp 112-124). Concentrations tend to be worse in the winter months.

Lead

Lead is highly toxic, causing damage in particular to the brain and central nervous system. Acute lead poisoning is now rare, and instead concern now focuses on the way consistent low-level exposure impedes the mental development of children – see pp 7-12 under drinking water.

Air pollution is another important source of lead intake in children. They inhale air and dust containing it, and may also suck fingers and objects contaminated by fall-out. Airborne lead comes mainly from motor vehicles, although some also stems from coal combustion and certain metal works. Since the 1920s lead compounds principally tetra-ethyl lead have been added to petrol to prevent 'knocking'. They retard combustion so that the fuel does not explode violently and damage the engine. After the petrol is burnt in the engine most of the lead it contained is pumped out into the atmosphere through the exhaust.

Lead in petrol has been responsible for much of the lead in the air we breathe, and for large quantities of lead particles in urban dust. Concentrations are naturally particularly high near busy roads, but the pervasiveness of the motor vehicle means that distribution is widespread. Lead in air and in dust also contaminates soil, crops and animal pasture and therefore further increases human lead intakes through the food chain.

Levels of airborne lead have been falling due to gradual reductions in the 1980s of the levels allowed in ordinary petrol and also increasing use of lead-free petrol. These measures followed energetic campaigning by environmental groups.

In the UK the maximum permitted level of lead in petrol was reduced from 0.84 g/l (grams per litre) in 1970 to 0.45 in 1976, 0.4 in 1981 and 0.15 in 1985 (Haigh, 1990, p208). Unleaded petrol has been available since 1986. Initially its impact on the market was minimal, but since 1989 its availability and use has rapidly increased so that in 1991 it constituted 43 per cent of petrol deliveries (DoE, 1992a, p15). Since October 1990 all new vehicles must be able to run on it.

These measures have brought about dramatic benefits. In 1990 estimated lead emissions from road vehicles were only 27 per cent of the 1975 figure (DoE, 1992a, p13). However the problem has not been entirely eliminated and further reductions in such emissions are desirable.

Petrol is not the only source of airborne lead which matters. In some localities other factors are important. For example in 1989 a copper recovery plant in Walsall was emitting high quantities of lead which brought local concentrations in the air above the EC limit (Her Majesty's Inspectorate of Pollution, 1990, p8).

Benzene

Benzene is a known carcinogen which is contained in petrol. In the air it stems mainly from motor exhaust emissions and evaporation of petrol during distribution and sale. More than one study has suggested that benzene from petrol could be causing increased rates of childhood leukaemias in areas with high levels of car use, but this hypothesis is not popular with most scientists researching the causes of such cancers (*The Times*, 9 April 1992; *The Independent*, 16 April 1992; Read, 1991, pp 28-30, 41). Benzene pollution from petrol is controlled much more tightly in the USA than in Europe, and information on its prevalence in the UK atmosphere is scant.

Dioxins

This term refers to a large group of closely related chemical compounds. They are widely considered to include the most toxic chemicals in existence, although there are some scientists who question their ability to damage seriously human as opposed to animal health.

Dioxins are formed during the combustion of organic compounds containing chlorine, such as PVC (polyvinyl chloride). The main source in the UK is waste incineration, mainly from municipal incinerators, but also from factory, hospital and commercial toxic waste incinerators. They are also produced by coal burning, vehicle exhausts and certain industries. Minute trace levels are found widely in the UK environment (British Medical Association, 1991, p112). Atmospheric emissions result in deposits in soil and surface water, and they can then build up in the food chain.

Dioxins affect living beings in a variety of ways and their impact on human health requires further research, but it seems that children are more vulnerable. A review of the human toxicity of polyhalogenated biphenyls (PHBs), a chemical category which includes dioxins, concludes that 'the developing human is more severely affected by PHBs than is the adult' (Lambert and Hsu, 1992, p185). Dioxins are also known to affect the thymus gland in the neck which is particularly important for the functioning of the immune system in young children (Allen, 1992, p198).

According to the Women's Environmental Network (WEN), between one and eight per cent of children in the UK may be suffering 'diminished potential' because of dioxins and related chemicals. This includes poorer reflexes, muscle tone, responsiveness and short-term memory, with possible implications for intelligence in later life. The argument is based on comparing dioxin levels in individuals in the UK to those in two studies in the USA where these effects on the central nervous system were found to be associated with maternal exposure to such chemicals before the children were born (Link, 1991, pp 82-8, 96).

Concern has also been expressed about the accumulation of dioxin in breast milk, since many chemical compounds ingested by a mother pass into her milk. In Britain the average breast-fed baby receives a daily quantity of dioxin 100 times the government's guideline level (Timberlake and Thomas, 1990, p104). However the levels are still minute and it does not make breast feeding less healthy than bottle feeding.

'Cocktail' effects

So far this chapter has looked at individual air pollutants, but modern British air invariably contains a combination of them. The proportions of the mixture (and the inclusion of other pollutants) vary from time to time and place to place.

It is difficult to isolate the health impact of each gas, but it is even more difficult to discover the 'cocktail' or 'synergistic' effects of mixing them. So far only limited research into this has been carried out, but some studies suggest that various pollutants may have greater impact when present together, for example ozone and sulphur dioxide. An American study found greater airway reactivity (the tendency of the airways in the lung to narrow) among 12 to 18-year-old asthmatics exposed to sulphur dioxide who had previously been exposed to ozone (Koenig et al, 1990; see also Holman and Festing, 1991, p20).

These potential cocktail effects require further investigation.

Smog

Smog is caused by a combination of pollution and weather conditions. It occurs when there is a 'temperature inversion' and cold, damp air at ground level is trapped by warmer air above. This prevents pollutant gases from dispersing and smog is formed. It results in much higher concentrations of pollutants and is therefore particularly threatening to health.

The smogs prior to the 1956 Clean Air Act involved smoke and sulphur dioxide as the main pollutants. Today the main component is likely to be nitrogen dioxide. Smogs still occur in Britain but are less dramatic to the eye because today's pollutants do not reduce visibility in the extreme way that large quantities of smoke did. For example in December 1991 London and several other cities were hit by smog which featured high concentrations of nitrogen dioxide. Hospitals reported increased numbers of children with lung problems and parents were advised to keep babies away from busy roads (*Sunday Times*, 15 December 1991).

Photochemical smog is a different kind of haze. This is caused by nitrogen oxides and hydrocarbons, emitted by car engines, reacting in the presence of sunlight to create ozone and a variety of organic compounds which condense in the air. It also occurs sometimes in British cities – for example there were episodes in May 1992 – but not as frequently or severely as in warmer parts of the world, most notoriously Los Angeles and Athens.

Smogs increase the threat which air pollution poses to health and therefore reinforce the need to tackle levels of the pollutants involved.

Local air pollution

In many areas air quality problems are caused by particular local industrial plants. There are a large number of factories in the UK capable of serious pollution. HM Inspectorate of Pollution, which regulates the most polluting industrial processes in England and Wales, oversees around 5,000 plants (although they do not necessarily all affect the air). Some plants have been the focus of particular concern and local campaigns.

In 1991 legal aid was granted to several families in Grangetown, Cleveland, to sue British Steel and ICI for health effects allegedly due to aerial emissions from the companies' plants (*Childright*, July/August 1991). The families are arguing that fumes from the plants are responsible for high local levels of asthma and respiratory problems in children. In some schools the headteachers keep a supply of inhalers to deal with asthma attacks. A community health study reported that almost every local health professional interviewed felt that industrial emissions must play a major role in local ill health (*Childright*, October 1990). The court cases are still pending at time of writing, but the decision to grant legal aid indicates that the families have at least 'reasonable grounds' for legal action.

In another case families in east London are suing the London

Docklands Development Corporation over disruption to their lives caused by major local building works. Their complaints include an increase in the numbers of GP consultations about children's respiratory problems (*Solicitors Journal*, 1 May 1992). It is argued that this is due to a massive amount of dust pollution stemming from the construction activity. Legal aid has also been awarded in this case.

Controversy has also surrounded the UK's four commercial hazardous waste incinerators, particularly the plant run by ReChem in Pontypool, South Wales. Local residents have complained forcefully about the site but the operators maintain there is no significant risk to health. Local mothers have formed a protest group, Mothers and Children Against Toxic Waste. Its Chair Sara Preece says: 'Mothers here are worried about their children being at greater risk of illness and danger than children in other areas' (*Children First*, Spring 1992). The three other existing hazardous waste incinerators are ReChem's other plant at Southampton, Cleanaway's in Ellesmere Port and Leigh Environmental's near Sheffield. Government and EC policy now encourages using incineration to dispose of toxic waste, and several applications to build new commercial incinerators are being considered by planning authorities.

Conclusion

The above analysis shows that in the UK levels of nitrogen dioxide, ozone, sulphur dioxide and carbon monoxide regularly exceed international guidelines aimed at protecting health. The exact impact of this is impossible to specify, but it is clear that because of their vulnerability children will be worse affected than adults. Numerous international studies have shown links between children's respiratory symptoms and diseases, and levels of air pollution. The evidence suggests that air pollution in the UK, mainly due to cars, is responsible for respiratory problems in many children. These include respiratory infections and breathing difficulties, and aggravating the difficulties of those who already suffer from lung diseases such as asthma and bronchitis. The health effects on children may well be greater in areas where there are industrial plants which contribute substantially to local air pollution.

In 1974 the Medical Research Council's Air Pollution Unit reported (see Children's Legal Centre, 1989): 'There is by now much evidence of an association between the general prevalence of respiratory illnesses in children and the amounts of pollution in the areas where they live'. Since then levels of some kinds of pollutants have fallen and others have risen. In 1990 Dr Jon Ayres, a consultant respiratory physician in Birmingham, told the British Thoracic Society that the level of respiratory problems was similar to that in northern cities prior to the 1956 Clean Air Act (*Environment Digest*, July-August 1990, p13).

An important current topic of debate is the extent to which air pollution causes asthma. This disease has become much more common in recent years, especially among children. The number of hospital admissions for childhood asthma increased fivefold from 1979 to 1989 (*The Independent*, 8 April 1992). The National Asthma Campaign estimates that one child in ten is now diagnosed as having asthma – it is the most common chronic disease of childhood. The increase in Britain is also reflected in other countries in the developed world.

The possible role of air pollution in this is uncertain, but there is much evidence to suggest that pollutants, particularly ozone, sulphur dioxide and sulphuric acid aerosols can trigger or aggravate asthma (summarised in Read, 1991, pp 31-39). In a recent study in Birmingham (Walters, Griffiths and Ayres, 1992) significant associations were found between hospital admission rates for asthma and respiratory conditions and both nitrogen dioxide levels (for all ages) and sulphur dioxide levels (for children under five). The authors state that this 'supports the hypothesis that air pollution may be a contributory cause for asthma'. Another recent study in Aberdeen (Ninan and Russell, 1992) suggests increased traffic fumes as a possible cause of an approximate doubling of reported childhood asthma between 1964 and 1989.

There is also anecdotal evidence: for example, a GP in the village of Godstone in Surrey has charted a dramatic rise in local childhood asthma since the M25 was built along its outskirts (*The Observer*, 26 July 1992).

Whether or not air pollution actually causes asthma in children and adults who did not previously have the disease, it certainly makes it worse for those who already do.

To protect the health of children further action is needed to monitor and reduce air pollution levels. The main need is to tackle air pollution from cars, which is now mainly to blame for the risk to children's health. This must include action to reduce the level of road traffic.

By January 1994 all new cars should have three-way catalytic converters which reduce emissions of carbon monoxide, nitrogen oxides and hydrocarbons, by transforming most of them into non-toxic substances before they emerge from the exhaust. This requirement was to have been introduced in January 1993 but the Government postponed it for a year.

The use of catalytic converters is a step in the right direction but far from a complete solution. Their efficiency is limited in low-speed, stop-start driving conditions. And their impact will eventually be counteracted by increasing road traffic, which the Government predicts will increase by between 72 and 121 per cent from 1990 to 2025 (Department of Transport, 1991a). This point is accepted by the Government, which says: 'In the longer term, however, much of the benefit of these measures [to reduce vehicle emissions] risks being lost through the continued growth in traffic volume and congestion' (DoE, 1992b, p101). According to Greenpeace calculations based on official figures, nitrogen dioxide levels in the year 2000 may be only five per cent less than 1983-84 and they will then rise (Greenpeace, 1992, p9).

Recommendations

- The European Community should adopt directives to cover *all* significant forms of air pollution.
- The Government should aim to meet all WHO guidelines for air quality as well as the binding EC directives.
- The Government should extend the air pollution monitoring network so that more detailed data is available. The system of air quality warnings should make clear the particular risk faced by children.
- All local authorities with environmental health responsibilities should monitor local air quality carefully and issue public health warnings when appropriate.

- The Government should make available more funding for air pollution research.
- The motor industry should conduct research into the benefits for children of all cars, like some lorries, having their exhausts at the top of the vehicle instead of the bottom.
- The Government and local authorities must take steps to reduce road traffic levels. This must involve more investment in public transport, better arrangements for cyclists and pedestrians, less road-building, encouragement of car sharing, and improved approaches to town planning.
- The Government should introduce a moratorium on the construction of new hazardous waste incinerators.

5. Ozone depletion and global warming

'Kids cook quick!'
Slogan used in Australian campaign to protect children from skin
cancer due to ultra-violet radiation (quoted in MacKie, 1992, p94).

The previous chapter dealt with polluted air which causes direct
health effects through entering children's lungs. This chapter
covers indirect effects which may stem from two major environmental consequences of air pollution: ozone depletion and global
warming.

Depletion of the ozone layer

The depletion of the ozone layer has health implications which
particularly concern children. These include increased risk of skin
cancer and possibly damage to the immune system.

The term 'ozone layer' and popular talk of 'holes' in it convey the
impression that somewhere in the atmosphere there is a thin veil of
ozone, punctured in various places but otherwise contiguously
encircling the earth. In fact it refers to a large portion of the
atmosphere, the stratosphere which is 12 to 30 miles above our
heads, where ozone, although still very rare, is at its most frequent.
These scarce and widely dispersed ozone molecules in the
stratosphere play a crucial role in absorbing harmful ultra-violet B
(UV-B) radiation from the sun, and thereby protect the earth and
its inhabitants.

However several kinds of gas created by human activity rise to
the stratosphere, react with ozone and lower its concentrations, at

least temporarily. This lets more UV-B radiation through. Scientists talk of a hole in the ozone layer when concentrations are down by 50 per cent or more above a particular part of the earth's surface.

The main chemicals involved in ozone depletion are: chlorofluorocarbons (CFCs) used as refrigerants, aerosol propellants and foam-blowing agents; halons used in fire extinguishers; and the industrial solvents carbon tetrachloride and methyl chloroform. Some scientists first became worried that these products might interfere with the ozone layer in the early 1970s, but it was the reporting in 1985 of massive ozone depletion over Antarctica which initiated major international concern.

These culprits are now being phased out under the Montreal Protocol, an international agreement on eliminating ozone depleting substances. However at the time of writing the UK is currently not aiming to cease their production until the end of 1995, and the Protocol itself in most cases lays down the year 2000. Furthermore even after production stops, the ozone layer will continue to get thinner for some time as depleting substances already in existence slowly rise through the atmosphere and react with the ozone. This will carry on into the next century.

Ozone fluctuates seasonally and each spring a hole has been appearing above Antarctica. Although this is the worst affected area for climatic reasons, ozone all around the globe has been suffering and levels above Europe are also being reduced. In 1991 it was estimated that they were down by 6 to 8 per cent. However in early 1992 data from the US space agency NASA and the European Arctic Stratospheric Ozone Experiment suggested ozone depletion over the USA and Europe is greater than previously thought. They estimated depletion of 15 to 20 per cent. The UK is therefore not exempt from the health risks of ozone depletion.

It has been estimated that a one per cent drop in ozone levels leads to a two per cent increase in UV-B radiation reaching the earth's surface (see Bridgman, 1990, p62). The longer people are exposed to this radiation, the more likely they are to develop certain forms of skin cancer, including malignant melanoma which is often fatal. The incidence of skin cancer has increased dramatically in the UK over the past 30 years, probably due to the growing popularity of overseas holidays. Fair-skinned people are much more likely to be affected. UV-B radiation can also cause cataracts and blindness.

Children are more vulnerable to the effects of UV-B radiation because their skin on the whole is more delicate, more likely to get sunburnt, and more likely to be damaged by the radiation. Exposure to UV-B radiation as a child makes malignant melanoma and other forms of skin cancer more likely as an adult. Some studies have argued that the crucial age range for exposure is 10 to 19, others that sunburn received when under 10 is particularly important (Elwood, 1989, p183).

Advice issued by the Government's Chief Medical Officer Kenneth Calman in July 1992 stated: 'Babies and children are particularly sensitive to strong sunlight. They should ... only stay in strong sunlight for very short periods'. This followed a recommendation from the official Committee on the Medical Aspects of Radiation in the Environment that warnings about the danger to babies and children needed to be reinforced (Department of Health, 1992a).

A Greenpeace report (Diffey, 1992) calculates that to counter the extra skin cancer risk due to ozone depletion British children would have to stay indoors between 11.30 am and 2.30 pm throughout a six-week summer holiday.

In Australia where skin cancer is very common and concern about ozone depletion is much greater, major publicity campaigns have been launched. Buckets of factor 15 sunscreen have been provided in schools to protect children when they go out to play (*Childright*, April 1992).

Concern has also been expressed about the implications of increased UV radiation for children's immune systems. It has been argued that the human immune system can be damaged by such radiation (for example see Haines, 1990, pp 156-7), and this could even result in children's vaccinations becoming counter-productive.

Vaccinations essentially involve giving an individual a mild form of the disease to be protected against. Vaccinating an individual whose immune response had been lowered due to exposure to ultraviolet radiation could actually make that person more rather than less susceptible to the disease (UNICEF/UNEP, 1990, p40).

However at the moment such threats remain speculative and more research is required.

The eventual health effects of ozone depletion are by no means certain but children do seem to be particularly affected. Further-

more protective measures now being taken by parents who follow
government advice are restricting the opportunities of children to
enjoy sunshine outdoors and to travel to spend their holidays in
sunny places.

Global warming

Carbon dioxide and various other gases in the atmosphere allow
light from the sun to pass through on its way to the earth's surface
but trap the infra-red radiation which the surface emits in response.
This is the 'greenhouse effect' and it keeps the earth warm enough
to support us and other forms of life. The scientific consensus is
that this is now going too far and growing levels of carbon dioxide
and other gases are trapping too much heat, leading to a rise in
global temperature.

Carbon dioxide is the main greenhouse gas but other significant
ones include methane, the CFCs which also deplete ozone, and
nitrous oxide. Water vapour also plays an important greenhouse
role. The problem stems mainly from the burning of fossil fuels in
power stations, industry and vehicle engines.

The direct health impact of global warming is difficult to predict,
but it seems likely that children will be particularly affected at least
in some ways. Children, particularly young ones, are less able to
adapt to extreme temperatures and would find the more frequent
very hot weather more difficult to cope with, especially in warmer
parts of the world (Timberlake and Thomas, 1990, p195; Haines,
1990, p151). Across the world it is likely to result in the spread of
infectious diseases which flourish in warm weather and to which
children are particularly vulnerable. However the direct health
effects are likely to be outweighed by the secondary effects from
other consequences such as coastal flooding.

The current generation of children may well have to live with the
future consequences of global warming, and when they are adults
it may be their children or grandchildren who suffer disproportionately. However at the moment it is not yet having a
major impact on the health of children in the UK.

Recommendations

- The Government and industry should ensure the elimination of all variants of ozone-depleting chemicals as soon as possible, ahead of the timings laid down in the Montreal Protocol.
- The Government should ensure more detailed monitoring of ultra-violet radiation levels, with the provision of more information to the public.
- The Department of Health, the Health Education Authority, and health authorities should reinforce efforts to inform children, parents and schools of the risks from UV radiation, and also of measures such as use of appropriate sunscreen and wearing of appropriate hats and clothes which minimise the risk without excessive interference with children's play opportunities and lifestyle.
- The Government, industry, local authorities, other organisations and individuals, as well as the international community, must take further steps to reduce creation of the greenhouse gases which lead to global warming.

6. Land and other pollution

'Polluted beaches have acquired the symbolic value of the poisoned apple, as something inherently wholesome which has become contaminated.'
(British Medical Association, 1991, p121)

Contaminated land

The UK has traditionally tried to get rid of most of its waste by dumping it in the ground. Currently there are over 4,000 landfill sites licensed for waste disposal (DoE, 1992a, p65). There are also thousands of disused sites. For many years the landfill industry was poorly regulated and in many cases little is known about the waste content or design of old sites. Currently these sites are unregistered and often unprotected.

Liquid can seep out of landfill sites and contaminate local land and groundwater. Depending on the waste in the site this liquid may contain toxic chemicals. There are frequent examples of children playing on badly managed current or disused sites, where they may ingest dangerous dust or soil. In one instance children were using as a play area a private waste tip in Gloucestershire where low level radioactive waste from a factory using radium to make luminous dials had been dumped (Children's Legal Centre, 1989).

In a particularly famous case in the USA, a school and housing estate were built on a disused waste disposal site called Love Canal in Niagara City, New York. This caused much controversy in the late 1970s about the impact on the residents of chemicals leaching from the site. An increased prevalence of non-specific symptoms such as skin rashes and headaches was reported among exposed children. One study attributed reduced growth in children born and living in the area to exposure to the site (BMA, 1991, pp 117-9).

Children here can also find themselves living on contaminated land. In 1991 a housing estate in Portsmouth was evacuated after the discovery that it was built on a site where poisonous waste had been dumped (Humber, 1992). In another case which came to notice in 1991, residents of a Kent housing estate were warned that local children could have increased blood lead levels because the estate had been constructed on a disused waste tip (Sabin, 1991).

Land can also be contaminated by other means, such as disused gasworks, chemical plants, power stations and a wide variety of industrial operations. Again children may play on derelict land or other places which are polluted for these reasons.

In 1988 Friends of the Earth publicised the case of an old chemical factory in Ilford, east London, which had used radioactive materials. The factory was demolished without the site being properly cleaned. Surrounded by a housing estate and overlooking a school, it was not properly fenced off and local children were using it as a playground. At certain spots it had radiation levels 50 times the normal background rate (Children's Legal Centre, 1989).

No one knows the extent of land contamination in Britain. At time of writing the Government is consulting on proposals under the 1990 Environmental Protection Act which would require local authorities to draw up registers of land most likely to be contaminated. Environmentalists have attacked these plans because only the worst forms of pollution are to be covered.

Dog fouling

This is a significant problem due to the estimated seven million dogs kept in Britain. Humans can catch the disease toxocariasis from a parasite, toxocara canis, found in dog faeces. The parasite's eggs can survive on the ground for months. In some cases the disease causes visual impairment and in extreme cases blindness. It may also lead to asthma and epilepsy and sub-clinical problems such as aches and pains. Children are more likely to be affected because they play on the ground in parks and other places which dogs frequent, and because young children may put soil in their mouths.

The annual number of toxocariasis cases is unknown, but it has been estimated that there are 100 to 200 cases a year of toxocara-induced eye disease, of which one or two result in complete blindness in one or both eyes (Ibarra, 1992). A 1981 study found that 14 per cent of children playing in an urban park had antibodies in their blood which indicated they had caught the infection at some point. Fortunately most of those who catch it do not suffer the most serious symptoms.

Spray drift

Children can be affected by direct contact with pesticides due to spray drift, when agricultural or other pesticide spraying accidentally reaches nearby roads, footpaths, public spaces, gardens or homes. Each year several complaints are made to the Health and Safety Executive (HSE) about children who have suffered for example from breathing difficulties, sore throats, and skin and eye irritation, due to spraying which has exceeded its target area (see for example HSE, 1992). However many people are unaware of the possibility of complaining to the HSE, and environmentalists argue that the official figures dramatically understate the number of spray drift incidents (Dudley, 1991, p188; Lang and Clutterbuck, 1991, p51).

Beaches

Children swimming in the sea at many of Britain's beaches face a threat to their health from raw or inadequately treated sewage.

According to the Government (DoE, 1992a, pp 36-7) 110 of the UK's 453 main beaches, 24 per cent, did not comply in 1991 with the bacterial limits laid down in the European Community's bathing water directive (EC, 1976). The worst affected region is the North West, where only two out of 33 beaches complied with the directive throughout 1988-91. Other areas which fare badly are Scotland, Northumbria and Southern (the regions are based on water companies). Seaside resorts which have a particularly bad record include Blackpool, Southport, Morecambe, Rhyl, Llandudno, Cleethorpes and Lyme Regis (National Rivers Authority, 1992, pp 49-59).

The Government deems beaches to comply with the EC

directive if they meet its requirements on the presence of coliform bacteria in total and also faecal coliform bacteria in particular. Coliform bacteria normally inhabit the colon or large intestine. Faecal coliforms are of faecal origin. Their presence indicates contamination by human or agricultural sewage. It also suggests the presence of other bacteria which are more difficult to measure and may be more harmful.

However, the directive also covers other forms of pollution, including salmonella bacteria and entero-viruses, viruses which normally inhabit human or animal intestines. It is clear from the data published by the National Rivers Authority (NRA, 1992, pp 60-70) that there are beaches which meet the coliform standards but fail to meet other standards in the directive. According to the Department of the Environment (personal communication), 175 of the 388 beaches tested in 1991 for entero-viruses exceeded the EC limit, and this also applied to 66 of the 429 beaches tested for salmonella. By relying simply on the measures of coliform bacteria the Government is substantially underestimating the number of beaches which fail to comply with the EC directive.

The main hazard from beach pollution is viral or bacterial infection, and children are especially at risk. The link between bathing in sewage-polluted water and disease is particularly strong in the case of children under five (Group of Experts on the Scientific Aspects of Marine Pollution, 1990, p54). The most likely consequences include gastro-enteritis, diarrhoea, nausea, vomiting, inflammation of the ear, nose and throat, and skin irritation (House of Commons Environment Committee, 1990). Children are also more likely to swim, paddle or play in the water at beaches and so come into contact with pollution.

A study carried out in 1990 by the Environmental Epidemiology Research Unit at Lancaster University confirmed the link between ill health in children and sewage pollution of beaches (Alexander et al, 1992). It found that of over 700 children between six and 11 who had visited Blackpool beach in the summer, those who had been in contact with the water were significantly more likely to suffer from vomiting, diarrhoea, itchy skin, fever, lack of energy and loss of appetite. Untreated sewage is pumped directly into the sea at Blackpool, which despite being Britain's most popular holiday resort also has one of the country's worst beaches. This is the only study which has looked specifically at children and beach pollution in the UK. Several other more general studies have linked ill health of this kind and sewage pollution of beaches.

It has also been claimed that more serious health effects have been caused. It was reported that in 1988 two boys became paralysed after contracting a viral infection on a school canoeing trip to Southend. Their parents and others blamed sewage in the water (Rose, 1990, p19).

The Coastal Anti-Pollution League, which campaigned strongly against beach pollution but no longer exists, was set up in 1957 by a father whose six-year-old daughter caught polio and died after bathing near a sewage outfall in the Solent. Although in the 1950s and 60s sewage presented a risk of polio and typhoid, this is now much less likely due to vaccination programmes.

The pollution is caused by the discharge of sewage, some treated and some raw, into the sea. This is widespread around Britain's coasts. The sea should disperse it, and sunlight and saltwater help to kill the harmful micro-organisms. The problem occurs where the pipes, many built in Victorian times, do not go out far enough from the shore and sewage is washed back. This is now being tackled through a programme of introducing longer outfalls and extra sewage treatment. The UK Government's aim is to bring the vast majority of beaches in line with the EC directive by the mid 1990s and all of them by 1997. The directive's implementation date was 1985.

The European Community also sponsors the 'Blue Flag' scheme for the best beaches. To receive a blue flag award beaches have to meet all the microbiological standards in the directive, along with some other criteria such as provision of facilities. In 1992 only 17 British beaches received the award (*The Guardian*, 5 June 1992).

Inland waters

A beach is covered by the EC directive if it is designated by the Department of the Environment as a popular bathing area. Unlike other countries, the UK Government has not designated any inland waters. Nevertheless many rivers, lakes and canals are used for swimming and water sport, and contact with polluted fresh-water can involve similar health risks to those from beaches. A further hazard may stem from toxin-producing algae that can grow in waters containing excessive nutrients, usually due to agricultural activity and sewage (this is called 'eutrophication'). Polluted rivers have also been linked to cases of Weil's disease or leptospirosis, a feverish disease transmitted through rat urine.

In June 1992 the Royal Commission on Environmental Pollution (RCEP, 1992) reported that freshwater quality in England and Wales had generally deteriorated over the past ten years. The Commission called for monitoring of the microbiological quality of water at sites where bathing or water sports are common, so that information on the presence of disease-causing micro-organisms would be publicly available.

Recommendations

- The Government and local authorities should ensure that contaminated land is publicly registered and that until cleaned up it is properly protected.
- Local authorities should expand education campaigns about dog fouling aimed at dog owners, parents and children; introduce by-laws requiring that when owners are out with their dogs they have with them and use the means to clear up the mess left behind; appoint additional dog wardens; and create more properly enforced dog-free areas in parks.
- The Government should ensure better monitoring of spray drift incidents and enforcement of measures designed to prevent them.
- The Government and the water industry should make sure that the country's beaches comply as soon as possible with all the parameters laid down in the EC directive.
- The Government, the National Rivers Authority and the water industry should ensure that freshwater sites commonly used for bathing and water sports also meet the full requirements of the EC directive.

7. Radiation

> 'Children, both before and after they are born, are particularly sensitive to
> ionizing radiation. High doses of radiation can kill cells, damage organs
> and cause death quickly. At low doses, radiation can initiate only partially
> understood chains of events which lead to cancer or genetic damage. The
> damage done by high doses normally appears within hours; that done by
> lower doses may take many years to emerge'.
> (UNICEF/UNEP, 1990, p21)

Children's health can also be affected by some forms of radiation,
an omnipresent feature of our environment.

Radiation varies from radio waves and sunlight to the sub-atomic
particles emitted by radioactive substances. It is a general scientific
term which means the emission of energy in the form of particles
or waves. In discussions of its implications for health it is invariably
divided into two kinds – ionising and non-ionising. Ionising
radiation possesses enough energy to remove electrons from atoms
and thereby ionise them. Everyone acknowledges that it can
damage human cells and is therefore dangerous. Some have argued
that various forms of non-ionising radiation in the environment
also pose a threat, but this is far from being generally accepted.

Ionising radiation

This includes cosmic radiation from space, sub-atomic particles
emitted by decaying radioactive materials, and the high frequency
end of the electro-magnetic spectrum – gamma rays, X-rays and
some ultra-violet radiation.

Much natural background ionising radiation occurs in our
environment, such as cosmic rays and radioactive radon gas (which

can concentrate inside buildings) released by naturally occurring uranium in rocks and soil. This natural level has been increased by human activities, including the use of X-rays in medicine, fallout from nuclear weapons testing, and certain industries, as well as nuclear installations which produce radioactive by-products.

Ionising radiation disrupts atoms by removing electrons from them. This results in the formation of highly reactive particles which can cause damage to living cells and tissues. Large doses of ionising radiation (like those suffered by some firefighters at Chernobyl) can kill outright, while lesser but substantial doses may cause immediate radiation sickness and severe ill health. However, short of a major accident at a nuclear installation or nuclear war, children in Britain are unlikely to receive such doses – the largest doses are received by those undergoing radiotherapy because they are already seriously ill. The important issue is the health risk involved in exposure to low doses.

The most serious threats from low-level radiation are cancer and genetic mutation. It is thought that ionising radiation reacts with body tissues in a way which creates cells with DNA abnormalities which are thereby predisposed to cancer and genetic defects (Simpson, 1990, p40). However the mechanisms involved are not fully understood yet. The effect of radiation stems from the reproduction of cells thus damaged. The cancers may not show up until many years after the radiation is received and genetic mutations will not be apparent until future generations. Leukaemia, a cancer which affects the white blood cells, is one of the more common consequences of irradiation. One form of the disease, acute lymphoblastic leukaemia (ALL), occurs predominantly in children.

A growing child is more vulnerable to radiation than adults (and the child in the womb even more so). For example, small doses of radiation to a child's cartilage can slow or halt bone growth or cause deformity. The younger the child, the more severe the stunting. Irradiation of children's brains during radiotherapy has caused changes in character, loss of memory, and dementia (Elsworth, 1990, p385).

Children from Hiroshima and Nagasaki who were under ten at the time of the bombing now show an excess risk for all cancers (except leukaemia) eight times greater than survivors who were over 35 at the time. In the case of leukaemia the excess risk is four times greater (Radford, 1987, p94). Similar evidence comes from the Marshall Islands in the Pacific which were affected by fall-out from nuclear weapons testing in 1954. Islanders under 20 at the time are much more likely to have since developed thyroid disorders including cancer than older people (Merke and Miller, 1992, p147).

Ionising radiation clearly is potentially harmful. Environmentalists argue that there is no threshold below which exposure can be considered safe, in that any radiation increases the chance of cancer. Official safety limits have been dramatically reduced over the years.

Some sources of ionising radiation such as cosmic rays from space cannot be prevented. In other cases such as medical X-rays the health benefits should outweigh the risks. It makes sense not to add unnecessary exposure to radiation, even if it is comparatively small, to exposure which is either inevitable or judged to have counteracting benefits.

Nuclear installations

The most well-publicised and controversial aspect of the relationship between ionising radiation and children's health has been the excess rates of leukaemia in the vicinity of some nuclear installations. This has been the subject of several official reports as well as a vigorous dispute between environmental organisations and the nuclear industry. The excess clearly exists, but the difficulties have been firstly to assess whether the nuclear plants are responsible and secondly, if they are, to identify the mechanism by which they are causing leukaemia. There are also other clusters in the UK which are not near nuclear sites and any rare disease such as leukaemia tends to cluster as a matter of statistical chance.

The possibility of a link between child leukaemias and the nuclear industry was first widely publicised in 1983 by a Yorkshire Television documentary. This found a rate of child leukaemia ten times higher than the national average in the vicinity of the British Nuclear Fuels (BNF) nuclear reprocessing plant and reactor complex at Sellafield in west Cumbria. This site reprocesses used nuclear fuel from other nuclear installations and discharges radioactivity (both intentionally with legal permission and sometimes accidentally through leaks) into the local sea and air. The Government commissioned Sir Douglas Black, former President of the Royal College of Physicians, to investigate. He confirmed the high level of leukaemias but said there was no proof that Sellafield was the cause (Black, 1984).

The Black Report led to the Government setting up the Committee on the Medical Aspects of Radiation in the Environment (COMARE), an independent advisory committee of medical and scientific experts. This confirmed the existence of high child leukaemia rates close to Sellafield and Dounreay – Britain's other nuclear reprocessing plant on the north coast of Scotland. It said (COMARE, 1988) the evidence probably supported the hypothesis that some feature of Sellafield and Dounreay had caused the excesses, but it added that on conventional estimates of their risk neither the authorised or accidental radioactive discharges were large enough to be responsible. Further research was therefore needed.

Another COMARE report (COMARE, 1989) found a small but statistically significant raised level of childhood leukaemias around Aldermaston and Burghfield, Ministry of Defence plants in Berkshire involved in the manufacture of nuclear weapons. It again said the known radioactive discharges were insufficient to explain the results and that further research was necessary. Claims have also been made about increased leukaemias close to other nuclear power stations, such as Hinkley Point in Somerset (see for example Urquhart, 1987).

In an important study published in 1990 a medical research team headed by Southampton University epidemiologist Martin Gardner reported a statistical connection between child leukaemias around Sellafield and exposure to radiation of fathers who worked at the plant (Gardner, 1990). Children of fathers who had radiation exposure above a certain level were six to eight times more likely to contract leukaemia. However this link only applied to some of the local children who had leukaemia, and the mechanism that would be involved has not been established. A similar study of the leukaemia excess around Dounreay found no link with paternal occupation at the plant there (Urquhart et al, 1991).

Although the evidence currently available suggests that the nuclear installations are linked to the excesses, the mechanism has not been identified and the causes are still subject to further research. At the time of writing several families from the Sellafield area whose children contracted leukaemia are suing British Nuclear Fuels for compensation.

Chernobyl

Children in the UK can also be exposed to radiation as a result of the activities of the nuclear industry elsewhere. The explosion in April 1986 at the Soviet nuclear reactor complex at Chernobyl was a powerful demonstration of this. The accident produced radioactive plumes which were then blown across Europe by the wind. Deposition of radioactivity was mainly dependent on rainfall, and the highest levels in the UK occurred in southern Scotland, Cumbria and north Wales. This led to official restrictions on the sale of sheep and lambs.

As a result of Chernobyl one-year-old children in the north of the UK were exposed on average to 0.9 milliSieverts (mSv) of radiation. The recommended maximum annual dose specified by the International Commission on Radiological Protection for members of the public is 1 mSv. Since the figure is an average, some children will undoubtedly have been exposed to significantly higher levels well above their recommended annual dose. It has been estimated that as many as 250,000 babies and young children in northern Britain could have exceeded their recommended annual dose in the aftermath of the Chernobyl accident (Elsworth, 1990, p86). It should also be noted that the dose limits have been attacked as too lenient by environmentalists. Friends of the Earth argue that to ensure no more than a 1 in 100,000 additional risk of death from cancer the annual public limit should be 0.3 mSv and that for children should be around 0.1 mSv (Green, 1992).

One of the main constituents of the Chernobyl fall-out was the radioactive element iodine-131 which, once in the body, travels like all forms of iodine to the thyroid gland in the neck. This means that children who received high doses are at greater risk of thyroid cancer, which can be fatal.

Radon

The biggest source of ionising radiation in Britain is not due to the nuclear industry but to radon, a naturally occurring radioactive gas which is released from small quantities of uranium in rocks and soil. It normally disperses in the air but can accumulate inside buildings. It has been estimated that exposure to radon could account for 2,500 deaths each year (DoE, 1992a, p45), but this figure is subject to a great deal of uncertainty. These deaths would mainly be due to lung cancer in older people, but there may also be a link between radon and childhood leukaemia.

Radon levels across the country vary according to the nature of the soil. High levels occur most frequently in Devon and Cornwall, which were declared 'radon affected areas' in 1990 by the National Radiological Protection Board (NRPB). These counties also have a noticeably high rate of acute lymphoblastic leukaemia (ALL), the kind which mainly affects children (Leeds University Centre for Clinical Epidemiology, 1990, pp 50-56). Of the counties covered in this survey, the only one with a higher rate was Cumbria, where Sellafield is located. In 1992 Northamptonshire and parts of Derbyshire and Somerset were also declared to be radon affected areas. At least some parts of Derbyshire and Somerset also have high levels of ALL (figures for the other parts and Northamptonshire are not available). This correlation between radon and ALL by county is at a rather crude geographical level and indicates the need for further research rather than demonstrating conclusive evidence of a connection.

On request the NRPB will arrange for radon levels in individual homes to be measured, but by mid 1992 only about 10 per cent of the 100,000 houses in the UK estimated to have high radon concentrations had been identified (*Which?*, July 1992). Local authorities are able to provide discretionary means-tested renovation grants for work to reduce radon levels, which can cost up to £1,000. However council spending on grants of this kind is minimal. In 1990 not one was paid by the district councils in Devon and Cornwall (Institution of Environmental Health Officers, personal communication). Many families with children are therefore either unaware of the risk to their health or unable to afford the work to their home necessary to minimise it.

Non-ionising radiation

Non-ionising radiation refers to less energetic electro-magnetic waves (with lower frequencies than ionising electro-magnetic radiation). It includes radio waves, microwaves, infra-red radiation, ordinary light and some ultra-violet radiation. Over the past century the extent of low frequency radiation has increased dramatically due to such features of modern life as radio and television broadcasting masts, mobile telephones, radar, domestic and office electrical equipment, and the electricity transmission network. Today we are all constantly bombarded by non-ionising radiation.

The issue of health risks from such radiation first achieved public prominence when it was reported in the 1970s that the Soviets had troubled the inhabitants of the US embassy in Moscow by 'zapping' the building with microwaves. Years later some women peace protesters at Greenham Common claimed that the US military were zapping them. Questions are now being widely raised about potential dangers, particularly but not only from the powerful extremely low frequency electro-magnetic fields created near major electricity transmission lines.

Concern has gone much further in the US than here, and some of it has focused on children. It was sparked off by research in Denver, Colorado which reported an increased incidence of childhood cancer in the vicinity of power lines (Wertheimer and Leeper, 1979). This was followed by other studies which reinforced the disquiet. In 1986 Houston Power and Lighting was ordered to pay $25 million in damages to the local school district for erecting a major power line within 60 metres of three schools. The line has since been moved (Goldsmith and Hildyard, 1990, p61).

In the UK in 1992 a National Radiological Protection Board review of the available evidence stated:

While there is suggestive evidence of an association between childhood cancer and residential electromagnetic field exposure, the methodological shortcomings of the studies are such that the evidence is insufficient to allow conclusions to be drawn.

It concluded that there was 'some weak evidence' associating childhood leukaemia with electromagnetic fields, but 'no firm evidence' (NRPB, 1992, pp 79, 133-5). It called for more research to be conducted.

The claim that childhood leukaemia can be caused by electro-magnetic fields is one of five hypotheses on the causes of childhood cancers currently being investigated by the UK Co-ordinating Committee on Cancer Research in a major five-year research project which began in 1992 (UKCCCR, 1992).

In Britain one author has argued that modern levels of electro-magnetic energy cause not only childhood cancers but also cot deaths. He states that his investigation of cot deaths in four London boroughs found a significant correlation with proximity to important sources of electro-magnetic energy (Coghill, 1990, pp 60-1). However his methods have been criticised. The Foundation for the Study of Infant Deaths has commissioned research in Avon to test the theory. The Foundation states (personal communication): 'No valid scientific evidence links electro-magnetic fields and cot deaths, but as the Foundation leaves no stone unturned we have asked a researcher to investigate'. At the time of writing the results of the research are not yet available.

At this stage the evidence on whether power cables and other sources of non-ionising radiation pose a health hazard to children is inconclusive.

Recommendations

• The nuclear industry should take further steps to reduce both radioactive emissions to the environment and the level of radioactive exposure of its workforce.

• The Government and local authorities in radon affected areas should give greater publicity to the threat posed by the gas.

• The Government should make contamination by radon a criterion for judging whether a property is unfit for human habitation.

• Local authorities should expand funding for grants for radon remedial work.

• The Government and relevant medical and scientific research bodies should ensure that further research is carried out into the possible health risks of non-ionising radiation.

8. Transport

'As recent studies have shown, children now lead increasingly confined and supervised lives and no longer walk or play on the street. Those that still do are at ever-increasing risk as more and more cars use our roads – some of them driven by parents taking children to school.'
Pedestrians' Association leaflet

The British transport system is dominated by road traffic. The car brings many benefits to children and adults, but it also has disadvantages, and these often affect children in particular. Air pollution has been discussed already; this chapter looks at some others.

Children's travel patterns

Table 1: Percentages of journeys over a mile long made by different modes of transport according to age

	Rail /tube	Car	Local bus	Walk	Cycle	Other
0-4	1	72	8	16	0	3
5-10	1	70	8	13	2	8
11-15	2	36	22	22	9	10
All under 16	1	56	14	17	4	8
16+	3	68	11	10	2	7
Total	3	66	11	11	2	7

(Source: Unpublished information derived from Department of Transport National Travel Survey 1985/6, personal communication)

As table 1 shows, 11 to 15-year-olds are far less dependent on the car for travel than other age groups. They make only 36 per cent of their journeys over a mile long in a car, whereas adults make 68 per cent and younger children make slightly more. Instead 11 to 15-year-olds make over half such journeys by walking, cycling or local bus – modes of transport which account for under a quarter of adult journeys. For transport planning to take account of children's interests it must provide properly for these three modes of travel.

I have limited this table to journeys over a mile because transport forecasting and policy-making usually relies on such figures – the data published from the Department of Transport's National Travel Survey generally ignores shorter journeys. If one does include journeys of less than a mile, a similar pattern still emerges of 11 to 15-year-olds relying much less on the car than adults, and much more on walking, cycling and local bus services (Potter and Hughes, 1990, p27).

The disregarding by the National Travel Survey of journeys under a mile means that the information base used to assist transport planning discriminates against children, since their journeys tend to be shorter than those of adults – 45 per cent of under-15s' journeys are less than a mile, compared to an average of 33 per cent for the whole population (Hillman, 1991, p19). The same unsatisfactory state of affairs applies to the later National Travel Survey carried out in 1988-91 , which is still unpublished at time of writing (Department of Transport Directorate of Statistics, personal communication).

International comparisons suggest that if cycling were made safer and more convenient, children would take it up even more. In Britain boys aged 11 to 15 make 13 per cent of their journeys by bike and girls four per cent. In the bike-friendly country of the Netherlands the figures for 12 to 14-year-olds are 61 per cent and 60 per cent respectively (British Medical Association, 1992b, p73). Cycling is especially important to children because it is the only form of mechanised transport they can use by themselves, yet it is grossly under-used in the UK.

In 1985-86 25 per cent of children lived in households without cars. This applied to 75 per cent in the lowest household income quarter (Department of Transport (DTp), 1988, p62).

It is also interesting to note that the Department of Transport officially values children's time as less valuable than the non-working time of adults, although the practical impact of this seems to be limited. In 1987 it published guidance (*Highways Economics Note No.2*) for the appraisal of proposed transport schemes in which it valued children's time as worth 47.6 pence per hour, compared to £1:27.4 for a retired person and £1:90 for the non-working time of a person of working age. (An adult's working time was valued at £7:24.8 per hour).

These figures do not appear in a later version of the guidance (DTp, 1989) which states instead: 'Where users are almost entirely children or pensioners, special values are available. These values, and advice about their use, should be obtained from [the Department of Transport]'. According to the Department (personal communication) it would still adopt values for children's and others' time in the same ratio as in the 1987 guidance, but it knows of no case since 1989 where they have actually been called into use.

Road accidents

The most dangerous feature of the outdoor environment is the risk of being knocked over by a car. The Government describes children as 'the most vulnerable road users of all' (DTp, 1990a, p1).

Table 2: Numbers of under-16s injured in road accidents in Britain in 1990

	Killed	Seriously injured	Slightly injured	Total casualties
Pedestrians	242	5,672	16,946	22,860
Cyclists	59	1,431	7,230	8,720
Car users	100	1,500	13,072	14,672
Others	16	267	2,105	2,388
Total	417	8,870	39,353	48,640

(Source: Adapted from Department of Transport, 1991c, p101)

As table 2 shows, in Britain in 1990 over 48,000 children under 16 were reported injured in road accidents. Of these 417 were killed and nearly 9,000 seriously injured. Over 39,000 minor injuries were also reported. Note also that there is substantial under-reporting of slight and serious injuries – the statistics are only based on police records (see for example British Medical Association, 1992, pp 48-9). Road accidents are the main cause of accidental death for schoolchildren. In 1990 they were responsible for 66 per cent of accidental deaths of five to 14-year-olds and 22 per cent of all deaths in this age group (DTp, 1991c, pp 18, 82, 104). Roughly one child in 15 can expect to be injured in a road accident before their sixteenth birthday (DTp, 1990b, p36).

Fifty eight per cent of those killed and 64 per cent of those seriously injured were pedestrians. The speed of the car is crucial to the seriousness of the accident. A car going at 20 mph which strikes a pedestrian is unlikely to kill or seriously injure; at twice that speed most pedestrians struck are killed (DTp, 1990a, p6). Most accidents involving children happen on local roads in built-up areas, so controlling car speed in residential areas is important.

Accidents are much more likely to happen to poor children. Where the head of household is in a professional occupation, the risk of a child being killed in a road accident is little more than half the average. For unskilled occupations it is nearly twice the average, and for the unemployed it is more than three times the average. A study by the Scottish Office also found that children with hearing disabilities were over 30 times more likely to be knocked down than children with good hearing (DTp, 1990a, p4).

Britain has a major problem of road accidents involving child pedestrians, which is recognised by the Government (DTp, 1990b, p36):

Great Britain's overall road safety record is one of the best in Europe, and for car drivers the number of fatalities per 100,000 vehicle kilometres is among the lowest. However the GB record for the number of pedestrians killed per 100,000 population is no better than average, and the rate per 100,000 population of child pedestrians killed on our roads is one of the worst in Europe.

The UK fatality rate for child pedestrians is 31 per cent higher than the EC average (Department of Transport, 1991b). In the case of ten to 14-year-olds, a comparison with the 19 other European countries for which figures are available shows only former Yugoslavia to have a worse record (Preston, 1992, p5). The

Government explains the high level of such casualties somewhat ungrammatically as follows (DTp, 1990a, p4):

Children in traffic are at greater risk of an accident than adults. Younger children in particular lack skill and experience, their observation and listening powers are less fully developed, their small stature, which means they are less likely to see and be seen, and their general immaturity of judgement all lay them open to danger in traffic. Older children are less likely to be supervised and may be influenced by their peers to take risks.

However it is also necessary to take account of driver behaviour. Research conducted at Nottingham University in the mid 1980s found that the presence of children at the kerbside had no effect on either the road positioning or the speed of drivers as they passed. One of the researchers stated that these findings are 'in flat contradiction to the retrospective evidence given when accidents have taken place' (when drivers claim they have taken all possible care or not seen the pedestrian before the accident) (see Lawson, 1990, p16).

According to a study of accidents involving young pedestrians in Birmingham, it was estimated that drivers were exceeding the speed limit in 46 per cent of 50 fatal accidents which occurred in 1983-88. In 18 per cent of cases they were exceeding the limit by over 10 mph (Lawson, 1990, p52). The author points out however that the child pedestrian is normally blamed for an accident by the police and others. He says (p125):

... those who report accidents on society's behalf (the Police) usually see young pedestrians as mainly 'at fault', as indeed does society itself ... Although the behaviour of young pedestrians will occasionally contribute to a road accident, drivers do not appear to acknowledge this in their driving, probably because the actual risk of an accident is very low. Society does not seem to be very critical of the conduct of drivers and so, when an accident occurs, unless the behaviour of the driver is atypical and extreme, it is the typical and often childlike behaviour of the young pedestrian where blame is directed.

When collisions occur their impact is likely to be more serious for children's comparatively fragile bodies. Children's bones are more pliant, so the force of impact is transmitted to their vital organs. Furthermore haemorrhaging tends to be greater, the higher up the body the injury is. So children are worse affected because they are shorter in relation to car heights (consultant accident and emergency surgeon quoted in *The Independent*, 31 March 1992).

The Government has published a proposed strategy to tackle the problem (DTp, 1990a). Its recommendations include extending traffic calming measures to enforce lower speeds in residential areas, and publicity and education campaigns aimed at drivers, parents and children.

Freedom of movement

Children's quality of life is affected not only by actual road accidents but also by fear of road accidents – generally their parents' fear of them. The UK's transport policy has been conducted with virtually total disregard for its impact on children's independent freedom of movement. The gradual extension of such freedom should be an essential part of growing up and maturing, but in Britain today it is seriously impeded by road traffic.

A unique and important study emanating from the Policy Studies Institute (Hillman, Adams and Whitelegg, 1990) has shown how in the past 20 years, a period during which traffic levels have nearly doubled, children's independent mobility has declined dramatically. The research was conducted in five disparate areas in England. It found that whereas in 1971 86 per cent of primary schools pupils aged seven to 11 went to school by themselves, in 1990 this only applied to 29 per cent. Similarly in 1971 63 per cent of these pupils were allowed to go to other places by themselves, but in 1990 this had dropped to 37 per cent. Large drops were also recorded in the numbers allowed to cross roads by themselves – from 72 to 51 per cent; and those with bicycles who were allowed to ride them on the roads – from 65 to 25 per cent.

The main reason given by parents for restricting their children's freedom of movement was danger from traffic. In the light of these figures it is not surprising that 77 per cent of parents stated that they had more opportunity to go out alone as children compared to children today.

The survey also found a stark and unexpected contrast with German children in demographically comparable areas. German parents are much more likely than English parents to allow their children to travel to school and other activities alone, cross roads by themselves, and ride their bicycles on roads. The authors suggest a number of possible explanations, including better recreational facilities for children and public transport, but state that they remain speculative pending further investigation.

The consequences of traffic danger for children's quality of life and their development are important. Of course children also benefit from being taken to places in cars but the downside is considerable. They have less freedom to experience and learn from independence and outside activities without adult supervision. Their play territory is reduced, so they have less chance to enjoy and explore their surroundings. They do less physical activity and are less fit as a result. In particular they cycle less often, although it is a healthy, environmentally sound and convenient form of independent transport. Furthermore traffic danger also results in an increased burden of adult supervision. This can mean that families, especially those living in cramped housing, are more likely to feel 'everyone is getting on top of one another'. It can therefore create more stress within the family.

Hillman et al conclude (p106): 'Our analysis suggests that the increase in personal freedom and choice arising from widening car ownership has been gained at the cost of a loss of freedom and choice for children ... The "personal freedom and choice" permitted a typical seven-year-old in 1971 are now not permitted until children reach the age of about nine and a half'. This aspect of children's development is therefore being set back for two to three years.

If the information were available then a comparison with say, 1920, would doubtless be even more dramatic than that with 1971. Colin Ward's classic work *The Child in the City* (Ward, 1978) contains much anecdotal evidence which illustrates the freedom of the city streets enjoyed by young children in times long past. Writing in 1978, Ward said:

The assumption that the car-driver has a natural right to take his vehicle anywhere has, quite apart from the threat to life, gradually attenuated many of the aspects of the city that made it an exciting and usable environment for children. The street life of the city has been slowly whittled away to make more room for the motor car ... Whole areas which were once at the disposal of the explorer on foot are now dedicated to the motorist. The city, which used to be transparent to young citizens who could follow the routes across it unerringly, is now opaque and impenetrable.

Children must be taught to recognise the dangers posed by traffic, but these should not be thought of as normal and inevitable. Instead their right to independent mobility should be recognised and an environment which allows this created – or perhaps recreated.

Other forms of transport

It should not be assumed that all other forms of transport apart from the car are automatically child-friendly. Public transport in Britain is often very inconvenient and stressful for adults transporting small children. A Gallup poll carried out in April 1992 found that parents of under eights are far from satisfied with transport services – see table 3. Trains, coaches, buses, railway stations, coach stations and bus stations were all predominantly thought to cater poorly or very badly for adults travelling with young children. Air and ferry travel fared somewhat better, but were generally regarded as adequate rather than very good.

Table 3: Opinion poll of parents of under-eights on transport services

When travelling with young children, how well do you think the following cater for your needs? (percentages)

	Very well	Adequately	Poorly	Very badly	Don't know
Trains	3	23	31	16	27
Coaches	1	19	33	15	32
Buses	2	23	39	20	16
Airlines	13	28	7	2	50
Ferries/ hovercraft	9	25	7	2	57
Railway stations	2	20	37	17	25
Coach stations	1	13	36	15	35
Bus stations	0	14	40	17	28
Airports	11	30	12	2	45
Ferry/ hoverports	4	20	11	4	60

(Source: *Gallup Political and Economic Index*, May 1992)

Contrast the experience here with the following description of public transport in Stockholm (Cavanagh, 1990):

The underground system or metro is almost entirely accessible with a pushchair. Every station has lifts from at least one entrance and there are simple metal or concrete tracks with handrails incorporated into staircases to allow carers with pushchairs to go up or down short flights of stairs ...

Swedish children's carriages are usually small prams and the larger type of pushchair which we used to use in Britain before the lightweight buggy became popular ... In Britain these prams and pushchairs would be regarded as a serious obstacle to mobility, particularly on public transport, so it was amazing for us to see two or three full-sized prams or pushchairs in a tube carriage. The tube trains and platforms are designed ... to be level on opening and to have almost no gap between door opening and platform.

At the central train station is further evidence that children's needs have been considered. A large well-equipped play area for waiting child passengers overlooks the main concourse which also has a baby feeding area and separate nappy changing facilities. Children are not expected to be left unsupervised but there is a seating area with books and magazines for carers and permanent receptionist who supervises the childcare facilities. Again there were lifts to all platforms and levels, and the long distance trains contained a children's play carriage, bookable in advance, adjustable in size according to demand, so carers and children may have a more enjoyable journey.

Buses being introduced now have air cushioned suspension, allowing them to drop level with the kerb at bus stops.

Although airlines are not so dimly regarded by parents of young children as other forms of public transport, they could also pay more attention to the needs of child passengers. In February 1992 a travel magazine accused airlines of providing 'woefully inadequate' facilities for children. Some airlines ban children from first class or, if they are in first class and they start crying, they are moved to economy class to cry there. So few facilities are provided for children that they may get up and play in dangerous areas. Nevertheless airlines charge for babies in arms who weigh no more than hand luggage (*Good Holiday*, March 1992).

British Airways bans children under 12 from its executive lounges (*Daily Telegraph*, 10 June 1992). It is difficult to think of any other category of human being which the company could discriminate against in this way and expect to get away with it.

Recommendations

- The Government and local authorities should adopt transport policies which: allocate public spending fairly to children's preferred modes of travel, including cycling, walking and local buses; ensure that their preferred and independent modes of travel are safe and convenient; promote children's right to independent freedom of movement; take account of children's opinions; and ensure that public transport has suitable access and facilities for children, including those with disabilities.
- Government transport statistics should include information about journeys which children make independently.
- The Government and local authorities should press ahead more urgently in introducing greater use of traffic calming measures such as 20 mph zones, speed bumps, chicanes, road narrowings, and mini-roundabouts.
- The Government should repeat and intensify driver education campaigns, particularly about the risks of driving at speed.
- Local authorities should promote cycling by creating more cycle routes, cycle paths on busy roads, and secure cycle parks.
- Local authorities should promote walking by taking pedestrian routes into account in new developments, ensuring pavements are wide and well-lit, and appointing 'pedestrian officers' to look at ways in which the life of the pedestrian could be made easier.
- Local authorities should encourage the location of new facilities where they are within walking or cycling distance for as many people as possible, and the location of new schools in particular should take into account the ability of children to travel to them safely and independently.

9. The built environment

'I read Lesley Garner's article (May 21) publicising the launch of your 'Parent Friendly' campaign with mounting irritation ... the prospect Miss Garner holds out of every new commercial or industrial building being purpose-designed to cater for an ingress of caterwauling delinquents and their ineffectual parents is dismaying indeed ... On the rare occasions one can escape from the demands of one's own children it is cold comfort to look forward to the pestilential attentions of other people's. If mothers (or fathers) accompanied by children wish to feel like 'respected human beings' they could start by appreciating that many of us have neither the time nor the inclination to spend our day in enforced dawdling caused by thoughtless parents intent on turning places meant for purposeful adult congress into makeshift playschools.'
Letter in *Daily Telegraph*, 22 May 1992.

If children are to benefit from the facilities provided for the whole community, these need to be physically accessible and convenient for them. Children also need sufficient and suitable recreational facilities of their own. Furthermore the planning process must take account of children's needs and views.

Design of buildings

No one has yet conducted a detailed national survey of public and commercial buildings to see how many present problems of accessibility and convenience for young children, especially those in prams and pushchairs. However such problems are undoubtedly widespread. (Sometimes staff attitudes to small children are as crucial as the physical attributes of the building but that issue is outside the scope of this book).

The features of a building which cause difficulties for young children and adults accompanying them (as well as many disabled children of all ages) are many and varied and include the following (for more details see Jaspert, Cavanagh and Debono, 1988, and Women's Design Service, 1992):

- doors, lifts and checkouts in supermarkets which are not wide enough to take a double pushchair;
- heavy doors which are difficult to hold open;
- automatic doors which do not respond to a small child's weight;
- doors which spring back;
- raised thresholds which children may trip over;
- lifts which close too quickly;
- absence of handrails at a child's height on staircases and ramps;
- escalators with no convenient lift alternative;
- turnstiles;
- glass doors with stickers only at adult eye-level;
- no public toilet facilities;
- children's facilities unnecessarily sited on upper floors;
- absence of comfortable and hygienic baby feeding and unisex changing facilities;
- absence of secure pushchair parks;
- display counters in self-service cafeterias which are too high for children to see or reach the food;
- counters in post offices and other shops which are inconveniently high for children to use.

It is clear from experience that many schools, hospitals, supermarkets, shops, shopping centres, leisure centres, hotels, railway stations, airports, motorway service stations and other buildings do not meet many of these requirements. To take supermarkets as an example, as part of its 'Parent Friendly' campaign the *Daily Telegraph* (5 June 1992) reported on five foodstores from major chains – Safeway, Sainsbury's, Tesco, Marks & Spencer and Waitrose – and found each of them sadly lacking in convenience for parents accompanied by young children.

Even where buildings are reasonably accessible they can be made more tolerable or sometimes pleasurable for children if they incorporate crèches, play areas or other amusements for children, especially where much time is spent waiting. Shopping centres and airports can have play areas; there is no reason why banks for example should not have minor amusements for children (as is often the case in some other European countries).

There is no excuse for new buildings which are inaccessible or inconvenient for young children and accompanying carers. Many of these features cost little or nothing when incorporated at the initial design stage. They can also often be introduced cheaply when buildings are in any case being modified. Fortunately awareness of these issues is spreading and designers of some new developments do strive to meet these points. Some shops such as the Swedish-owned furniture store IKEA have successfully made a marketing tool out of their child-friendliness.

Streets

Street pavements are another aspect of the built environment which often pose difficulties for young children in pushchairs and children who have disabilities. Problems can be caused by the following (Jaspert, Cavanagh and Debono, 1988, pp 7-9:

* street furniture such as bus stops, road signs, bollards, rubbish bins and post boxes which allow insufficient space for a pushchair or wheelchair to pass;
* narrow pavements;
* broken pavements and uneven surfaces;
* absence of ramps at subways;
* absence of dropped kerbs at crossings.

Road planning also generally prioritises the road user so that pedestrians trying to cross major roads are often forced into inconvenient detours down underpasses and over footbridges.

Play

One of the most important features of the built environment for children is the extent to which it includes enjoyable, stimulating and safe opportunities for play, which may or may not be dedicated children's play areas.

The previous chapter documented how children's freedom to explore their neighbourhood independently has been dramatically restricted. Nevertheless children still spend a substantial amount of their time in outdoor play. As they get older they are less likely to be supervised and more likely to roam further from their home, but the ages at which these developments happen are higher than in the past.

Children under 10 generally play within a few hundred yards of their homes (Parkinson, 1987, p6). In urban areas this often limits them to the streets, although where possible children tend to prefer playing in natural or wild spaces (Play Board, 1985). Older children also tend to spend most of their play time fairly close to home. Many urban neighbourhoods are short of suitable locations for children's spontaneous and non-organised play.

In rural areas problems of access to the countryside can also be created by the loss of public footpaths and the need to keep children safe from farm machinery and pesticide stores (for example see details of a survey in Humberside reported in Ward, 1988, p100).

As for designated play areas, the provision of such facilities is variable, badly funded and often inadequate. (The scope of this book is limited to environmental features such as playgrounds rather than services like out-of-school clubs, but the same point applies generally to them too).

Outdoor play facilities are often badly maintained, vandalised, in poor condition and sometimes dangerous. A Townswomen's Guilds survey in 1991 of 878 children's play areas found only one considered to be fault-free. The survey's disturbing results included that 68 per cent were badly maintained or littered, 39 per cent were fouled by dogs and 85 per cent of those near a road had no warning signs (Townswomen's Guilds, 1991). A Consumers' Association survey in 1988 (*Which?*, April 1988) judged only one in three of 139 playgrounds in Stockport, Great Yarmouth and Hackney to be safe. Frequent problems included bad design, poor maintenance, poor access, inadequate signs, litter and broken glass.

Provision in the UK is highly limited compared to many other European countries. For example, Rotterdam has five times the number of children's playgrounds likely to be found in a city of comparable size in the UK. In Denmark and Sweden the amount of space to be allocated to children's play in residential developments is three times the level which was advised by the Department of the Environment until 1981, since when there have been no government recommended standards for the provision of playspace (Coffin, 1989, p12).

Suitable facilities are often particularly limited for disabled children, for rural children in isolated communities and for poor children, such as those living on run-down housing estates.

A study carried out by the National Association for the Care and Resettlement of Offenders examined recreational provision on housing estates. It found (NACRO, 1988):

The level of social and recreational provision for children and young people on public sector housing estates in most areas is minimal. Many estates have no facilities at all. Others have limited facilities for perhaps one age group. Very few have an adequate range of facilities for all ages.

The report concludes that most planners 'have failed to plan for children and were principally concerned with protecting the environment from children and young people rather than including them in it'.

Play and recreation is vital to children's development and physical, mental and social well-being. All neighbourhoods should have a range of play provision – children should be able to play safely near their homes with friends.

The planning process

Most local authorities do not consult children as a specific group as part of the planning process. Surveys in 1989 (*Childright*, April 1989, and July/August 1989) found that only 20 per cent of London council planning departments said they had consulted children as a specific group, and 14 per cent of councils outside London said the same.

However where this had been done it was generally regarded as successful by the authority. For example Walsall reported that it had implemented proposals made by pupils for improving derelict land close to a school and this was 'very successful'; Manchester described children's involvement in designing a new park aimed to meet the needs of local children as 'very rewarding for the planning department'. On the other hand several said the key problem in consulting children was that there was no representative organisation for them.

Failure to consult children constitutes a breach of Article 12 of the United Nations Convention on the Rights of the Child, which says:

States Parties [states which like the UK have ratified the Convention] shall assure to the child who is capable of forming his or her own views the right to express those views freely in all matters affecting the child, the views of the child being given due weight in accordance with the age and maturity of the child.

An interesting new approach to planning for children has been adopted by Leicester City Council. It has decided to develop a 'child audit' approach to all planning applications and proposed changes to the road system. It also intends to establish a small number of 'play streets' where cars are banned and carry out research into creating zones where child pedestrians have priority over motorists (Leicester City Council, 1992).

Recommendations

- The Government should change building regulations so that new public buildings are required to be accessible and convenient for young children and accompanying carers.
- Local authorities should take account of the accessibility and convenience of developments for young children and carers in making planning decisions.
- Developers of new buildings to be used by the public should ensure that they are accessible and convenient for children and carers, and where feasible owners of existing buildings should ensure they are improved, especially when buildings are being modified.
- A general symbol to indicate pushchair access should be adopted widely, like the wheelchair access symbol. (Since a double pushchair is wider than a wheelchair, spaces that accommodate double pushchairs will also accommodate wheelchairs but not necessarily vice versa).
- Local authorities should ensure that children's play needs are catered for in new housing developments, shopping areas and public facilities, and that where possible existing but inadequate provision is updated. Planners must also take account of the need for children to experience and enjoy open spaces and natural areas.

- The Government should ensure that a national survey is carried out on the extent and quality of current play provision.
- Local authorities should take into account the views and needs of children in the planning process. Children should be involved in the consultative process for all planning decisions, not just those relating directly to play facilities, since they travel, shop and so on, like everyone else. Consultation also has to be directly with children, not by simply seeking the views of parents and teachers.
- Local authorities should appoint an officer with the specific responsibility of ascertaining the views and promoting the interests of children in the planning process, and assessing all proposals in terms of their impact on children. In Norway all municipal planning authorities must have such a person (Flekkøy, 1991, p145).

10. The indoor environment

'I don't think my gran and mum should smoke in my bedroom because it is the only private place I have and it is my choice whether I want it smoky or not.'
Twelve-year-old girl from Lothian (quoted in Michell, 1990, p45)

The main theme of this book is how the outdoor environment affects the quality of children's lives in the UK. However it would not be complete without some indication of the role of the indoor environment (household radon has already been discussed under radiation).

Passive smoking

Environmental tobacco smoke or passive smoking is the most important indoor pollutant. It is a significant health risk for many children.

In a 1990 study of children aged 11 to 15 carried out by the Office of Population Censuses and Surveys (OPCS), 33 per cent in England reported that their mother smoked and 36 per cent that their father smoked. In Wales the figures were 35 and 38 per cent respectively, and in Scotland both were 39 per cent (Lader and Matheson, 1990, pp 50, 54-5). Some children also lived in houses where siblings smoked. For technical reasons the survey results do not reveal how many children lived in a house where someone smoked. However a smaller survey of 658 10 to 14-year-olds in Lothian found that six out of ten live with at least one person who smokes (Michell, 1990, p28). The other figures for smoking prevalence in this survey are similar to the OPCS results for

Scotland, although on the whole slightly higher. We can certainly say that most children in Britain share their homes with at least one smoker.

Not surprisingly children are more likely to be regular smokers themselves or to have tried smoking if at least one of their parents smokes. For example in England children whose parents both smoke are two and a half times as likely to be regular smokers as those where neither smokes (Lader and Matheson, 1990, p51).

But despite this there are many children who do not smoke who are living in households where their parents do. Taking children both of whose parents smoke, in England 85 per cent do not smoke themselves and 51 per cent have never smoked. In Wales the figures are 87 per cent and 50 per cent, and in Scotland 82 per cent and 39 per cent. The percentages are higher where only one parent smokes (Lader and Matheson, 1990, pp 55-7).

This means that many children who have resisted the pressure to smoke, including the example set by their parents, are breathing in the environmental tobacco smoke their parents are creating.

Children may also experience passive smoking in other locations, but due to the amount of time they spend at home it is much more significant there. The risks of passive smoking are greatest in an enclosed space with smokers for a prolonged period. Children whose parents smoke cannot avoid this sort of atmosphere, even when they object strongly. The Lothian survey found that 58 per cent of 10 to 14-year-olds who had a smoker in the family thought that no one should smoke in their home (Michell, 1990, p36).

The effects on children of passive smoking have been summarised recently by the Royal College of Physicians (RCP, 1992, pp 9-23). Their report argues that 'the respiratory system of the young child is particularly vulnerable because it is structurally and immunologically immature and is developing rapidly'. Its conclusions include:

- Children of parents who smoke inhale the same amount of nicotine as if they themselves smoked 60-150 cigarettes a year.
- The children of smokers are more likely to suffer respiratory diseases such as bronchitis, pneumonia and bronchiolitis; more frequent and severe asthma; and ear, nose and throat problems such as 'glue ear', the commonest cause of deafness in

childhood. They also tend to be shorter, and are more likely to suffer from chronic lung disease and cancer as adults.

- Parental smoking is responsible for at least 17,000 admissions to hospital each year of children under five.
- Maternal smoking is associated with greater risk of cot death.
- Children of smokers are more often absent from school, so their education is affected.

Over the 1980s the health implications for children of passive smoking have been increasingly well understood, and they were recognised by the Government in the 1992 health White Paper (Department of Health, 1992b, p117).

Housing conditions

Housing conditions strongly influence the indoor environment and children's health. For example, an important study of over 1,100 children in Glasgow, Edinburgh and London found that those living in damp conditions are more likely to suffer respiratory problems such as wheezes, sore throats and runny noses, as well as headaches and fever. This took into account possible confounding factors such as household income, unemployment, overcrowding and smoking. Thirty one per cent of the dwellings surveyed, which were all council housing, had damp and 41 per cent mould growth. The authors conclude: 'Damp and mouldy conditions have an adverse effect on symptomatic health, particularly among children' (Platt et al, 1989; see also Furley, 1989, pp 10-17, and Whitehead, 1988, pp 297-9, for details of other studies linking poor housing and health). Housing conditions also affect children's emotional state and educational performance.

The 1986 English House Conditions Survey found that households with children were disproportionately likely to live in dwellings which were unfit for human habitation or in serious disrepair (DoE, 1988, p136). The situation is getting worse. The 1986 survey estimated that there were 900,000 unfit dwellings. The following survey, carried out in 1991, has not been published at time of writing, but according to DoE internal documents leaked to the press it will report an increase to over 1.3 million unfit homes (*The Independent*, 1 August 1992).

The special difficulties faced by children of homeless families placed in bed and breakfast accommodation have been well-documented (see for example Conway, 1988). Such accommodation is often overcrowded, insanitary, unsafe, lacking facilities and in poor repair. This naturally has serious consequences for the physical and mental well-being of the children who live in it, including infectious diseases, infestations, injuries, poor nutrition, behavioural problems and impaired development.

Tower blocks are particularly ill-suited for children. There is the constant danger that a young child may fall from a window or balcony, down the stairs or a rubbish chute, and fatal accidents have occurred. The need to keep young children under close adult supervision means they go out less, have less stimulation, mix less with other children, and their development is hindered (Clarke, 1992, p121).

Although the unsuitability for children of high-rise living is generally recognised, large numbers of children live in tower blocks. Many local authorities have had a policy of not placing children above a certain floor, usually the fourth or fifth, but the lack of public housing has made this an increasingly difficult policy to maintain. Sometimes the alternative to high floor flats is bed and breakfast.

Accidents in the home

Many homes contain dangerous features for children. In 1989 194 under 15s in England and Wales were killed in accidents in the home. The most common cause was fire, responsible for 88 deaths (Department of Health, 1990, p19). It is estimated (Department of Trade and Industry, 1992) that in 1989 1,080,000 under 15s in the UK were injured in accidents in the home which resulted in visits to hospital. The most common injuries were cuts or lacerations. However in five per cent of cases the child spent at least one night in hospital.

Dangerous features of homes can include unprotected staircases and balconies, glass doors, poorly stored hazardous medicines or cleaning products, hazardous cooking equipment, unsafe electrical equipment, unguarded fires and badly made furniture. This issue is well covered by the Child Accident Prevention Trust, whose publications should be consulted for further information.

The school environment

Children also spend a large amount of their time at school, and here too the physical environment can sometimes be unsatisfactory, dangerous or inaccessible.

Many school buildings are inadequate or in a poor state of repair. A 1986 Department of Education and Science (DES) survey found for example that 38 per cent of primary schools needed work done to roofs or heating systems and 32 per cent to walls and windows. The overall cost of bringing school buildings up to an acceptable standard of quality was estimated at £2 billion at 1987 prices. The results of the 1986 survey were broadly confirmed by a study carried out in 1990 for the National Audit Office (NAO).

These deficiencies impede the process of teaching and learning. To quote the NAO:

The adverse effects on the quality of education caused by buildings which are unsuitable for current educational demands, and badly maintained accommodation as identified in various surveys, have been repeatedly confirmed in reports by Her Majesty's Inspectorate of Schools. For example in 1984 the Inspectorate noted a statistically significant association between different standards of accommodation and the quality of work produced ... Poor accommodation was considered by the Inspectorate to be adversely affecting the quality of work in just over one-fifth of all the lessons seen. And in 1986 they reported that grim neglected buildings adversely affected morale and did nothing to stimulate and encourage pupils to give of their best (National Audit Office, 1991, p17).

The Inspectorate's annual reports since have reinforced the same message.

In 1989 the Elton enquiry into school discipline, initiated by the DES, reached similar conclusions about the importance of the school environment. It argued that a pleasant and well-maintained school environment resulted in better pupil behaviour. For example it praised the effect on a school's atmosphere of having areas with carpets (DES, 1989, pp 115-9).

The Health and Safety Executive estimated that around 75 accidents resulting in major injuries occurred in schools in 1989-90 due to poor maintenance or repair (NAO, 1991, p19).

Many older schools may have asbestos in their roofs, walls, doors, pipe lagging and many other parts of the building. It is sometimes found to be in a damaged and therefore unsafe state. Even in minute quantities airborne asbestos can cause mesothelioma, cancer of the membrane which lines the chest. According to the Health and Safety Commission, the risk of this 'is very much higher when exposure occurs early in life'. In numerous cases schools have had to be temporarily closed while the complex and expensive task of safe removal has been carried out.

Fluorescent lighting in schools has also been the subject of controversy. According to a study conducted by a consultant neurophysiologist at Birmingham and Midland Eye Hospital, children who suffered from migraine experienced reduced symptoms when they wore spectacles which blocked the flickering blue light emitted by fluorescent tubes (*The Independent*, 4 January 1992). Other studies have associated fluorescent lighting with headaches, eye strain and hyperactivity (*Childright*, October 1986).

Other dangers in the school environment can include hazardous chemicals used in teaching, unsafe electrical equipment, the use of dangerous cleaning materials, formaldehyde fumes given off by cavity wall insulation, drinking water affected by lead plumbing, and infectious diseases spread through poor sanitary facilities for pupils. Some schools are also affected by pollution from nearby industrial operations.

Many mainstream schools are inaccessible to pupils with disabilities. The problems usually involve lack of lifts and ramps, and unsuitable toilets. No national survey has been carried out to find out exactly how many schools present access problems for different kinds of disabilities. Even many local education authorities do not have this information for their own schools (Coopers & Lybrand, 1992, p14). Nevertheless it is clear that this is a major factor obstructing integrated education and restricting the choice of school available to pupils with disabilities.

Recommendations

- The Government, the Health Education Authority and health authorities should devote increased effort to public education campaigns to warn parents of the consequences for their children if they smoke at home.
- The Government and local authorities should devote more funding to house repairs to improve the condition of the housing

stock and also for new house-building for low income groups, and the Government should give authorities greater freedom to spend in this area.

- The Government and local authorities should make more money available for school building maintenance and for ensuring the integration of pupils with disabilities.

11. Conclusion

*'The well-being of children requires political action at the highest level. We
are determined to take that action.'*
Declaration issued by heads of government at the World Summit for
Children, New York, 30 September 1990

The preceding chapters show that children rather than adults are
bearing the brunt of pollution in the UK. Children are hit harder
by pollution because they are smaller, still developing and
physiologically immature. Generally their bodies are quicker to
absorb toxic substances and slower to eliminate them. Children are
therefore particularly badly affected by contaminated air, drinking
water, land and beaches.

In terms of the 'natural' environment the two problems which
affect the largest numbers of children are high lead levels in
drinking water and air pollution from road traffic. Many children
are drinking tapwater which has enough lead to damage their
intelligence. Large numbers of children across the country suffer
respiratory problems which in all probability are caused or
aggravated by traffic-related air pollution.

The indoor pollution problem which affects most children is
passive smoking, due to others in their household who smoke,
usually parents.

The built environment and transport system in the UK also often
fail to meet the needs of children, who have to cope with
inadequate facilities, inconveniently designed buildings, dangerous
roads and constraints on their freedom of movement. Children face
an environment which has predominantly been designed by adults
for other adults.

All this is not to deny important improvements which have happened over the past few years or are in the pipeline. The smogs caused by coal burning are now a feature of history; the gradual reduction of lead in petrol is slowly eliminating one of the major sources of this toxic chemical; measures to clean up drinking water and beaches are being taken to ensure compliance with European directives; traffic calming schemes are increasingly being introduced; more new buildings are being designed with children in mind. No matter that the government has generally been forced into action by environmental campaigners, public pressure and the European Community – these still represent real progress for the children of the UK.

But despite these and other steps in the right direction major problems remain. All too often children find their environment to be inconvenient, unpleasant, unhealthy or dangerous. The well-being of children in the UK is adversely affected by environmental factors which harm their health or stunt their development.

The following steps are the most important for tackling the major environmental obstacles to the health and well-being of the UK's children:

- lead in drinking water – a properly-funded rolling programme to eliminate lead plumbing in homes and public buildings, starting with the worst hit areas;
- air pollution from road traffic – measures to reduce road traffic, and to improve the systems for monitoring air quality and giving public warnings about air pollution;
- passive smoking in the home – public education campaigns aimed at persuading parents to stop or cut back on smoking at home because of the impact on their children's health;
- road safety and freedom of movement – more traffic calming schemes and other measures to make walking and cycling safer and easier, so that roads are safer for children and their opportunity for independent freedom of movement is increased;
- the built environment – extended opportunities for high quality, safe play, and changes to building regulations so that public buildings are accessible and welcoming for young children.

These are measures to deal with specific problems but more fundamental steps are also necessary to help ensure a good environment for children:

- The policy making process should pay greater attention to the impact of policies on children. This point goes wider than environmental issues. Elsewhere I have argued the case for creating a Children's Rights Commissioner, an independent and wide-ranging statutory office whose purpose would be to monitor the effects of national and local policy on children and to influence policy makers to take more account of children's interests (Rosenbaum and Newell, 1991). Comparable bodies exist at a national level in Norway and New Zealand. In Sweden there is a similar institution with a remit limited to environmental matters – the National Child Environment Council or Barnmiljørådet. This is a public body which promotes children's rights in the environment.
- Children should be given more opportunity to take part directly in the policy making process, so that their views are heard and listened to. This is in line with Article 12 of the United Nations Convention on the Rights of the Child, which requires that children's views on all matters affecting them should be given due weight.
- Assessments of the health effects of a particular polluting process should fully reflect its impact on children and other vulnerable groups, not just on healthy adults.

Bibliography

Adams, M., 1990, *Capital Killer: Air Pollution from Road Vehicles*. London: London Boroughs Association.

Advisory Group on the Medical Aspects of Air Pollution Episodes, 1991, *Ozone*. London: HMSO.

Alexander, L., et al, 1992, Symptomatology of children in contact with sea water contaminated with sewage, *Journal of Epidemiology and Community Health*, vol 46, pp 340-344.

Allen, R., 1992, *Waste Not, Want Not*. London: Earthscan.

Black, D., et al, 1984, *Investigation of the Possible Increased Incidence of Cancer in West Cumbria*. London: HMSO.

Bridgman, H., 1990, *Global Air Pollution*. London: Belhaven Press.

British Medical Association, 1991, *Hazardous Waste and Human Health*. Oxford: Oxford University Press.

British Medical Association, 1992a, *Pesticides, Chemicals and Health*. London: Edward Arnold.

British Medical Association, 1992b, *Cycling: Towards Health and Safety*. Oxford: Oxford University Press.

Broughton, G., et al, 1992, *Air Quality in the UK: A Summary of Results from Instrumented Air Monitoring Networks in 1990/91*. Stevenage: Warren Spring Laboratory.

Cavanagh, S., 1990, Thinking of small children in Stockholm, *WEB* (published by the Women's Design Service, London), Winter 1990.

Charpin, D., et al, 1988, Respiratory symptoms and air pollution changes in children: The Gardanne coal-basin study, *Archives of Environmental Health*, January/February 1988, vol 43, pp 22-27.

Children First, published by UNICEF-UK, London.

Children's Legal Centre, 1989, *Children and the Environment*. London: Children's Legal Centre.

Childright, published by Children's Legal Centre, London.

Clarke, F., 1992, *National Tower Blocks Directory*. London: National Tower Blocks Network.

Coffin, G., 1989, *Children's Outdoor Play in the Built Environment*. London: National Children's Play and Recreation Unit.

Coghill, R., 1990, *Electropollution*. London: Thorsons.

Committee on the Medical Aspects of Radiation in the Environment (COMARE), 1988, *Investigation of the Possible Increased Incidence of Leukaemia in Young People near the Dounreay Nuclear Establishment, Caithness, Scotland*. London: HMSO.

Committee on the Medical Aspects of Radiation in the Environment (COMARE), 1989, *Report on the Incidence of Childhood Cancer in the West Berkshire and North Hampshire Area*. London: HMSO.

Control of Pollution (Special Waste) Regulations 1980 (SI 1980/1709). London: HMSO.

Conway, J. (ed), 1988, *Prescription for Poor Health – the Crisis for Homeless Families*. London: London Food Commission, Maternity Alliance, SHAC and Shelter.

Coopers & Lybrand, 1992, *Within Reach: Access for Disabled Children to Mainstream Education*. London: Coopers & Lybrand.

Davis, M., and Grant, L., 1992, 'The Sensitivity of Children to Lead', in Guzelian, P., Henry, C., and Olin, S., (eds), *Similarities and Differences between Children and Adults: Implications for Risk Assessment*. Washington DC, USA: International Life Sciences Institute.

Department of Education and Science, 1989, *Discipline in Schools – Report of the Committee of Enquiry chaired by Lord Elton*. London: HMSO.

Department of Health, 1990, *Mortality Statistics – Accidents and Violence*. London: HMSO.

Department of Health, 1992a, *Advisory Committee Endorses Health Departments' Strategy on Skin Cancer, Ultraviolet Radiation and Health*, press notice H92/210, 1 July 1992.

Department of Health, 1992b, *The Health of the Nation*. London: HMSO.

Department of the Environment, 1988, *English House Conditions Survey 1986*. London: HMSO.

Department of the Environment, 1992a, *Digest of Environmental Protection and Water Statistics 1991*. London: HMSO.

Department of the Environment, 1992b, *This Common Inheritance – The Second Year Report*. London: HMSO.

Department of Trade and Industry, 1992, *Home and Leisure Accident Research – 1989 Data*. London: Department of Trade and Industry.

Department of Transport, 1988, *National Travel Survey 1985/86*. London: HMSO.

Department of Transport, 1989, *Highways Economics Note No. 2*. London: Department of Transport.

Department of Transport, 1990a, *Children and Roads: A Safer Way*. London: Department of Transport.

Department of Transport, 1990b, *Road Accidents Great Britain 1989*. London: HMSO.

Department of Transport, 1991a, *Cost-Benefit Analysis 9 Manual*. London: Department of Transport.

Department of Transport, 1991b, *Accident Fact Sheet No. 5: Child Casualties in Road Accidents*. London: Department of Transport.

Department of Transport, 1991c, *Road Accidents Great Britain 1990*. London: HMSO.

Diffey, B., 1992, *Stratospheric Ozone Depletion and the Risk of Non-Melanoma Skin Cancer in a British Population*. London: Greenpeace UK.

Drinking Water Inspectorate, 1992a, *Drinking Water 1991*. London: HMSO.

Drinking Water Inspectorate, 1992b, *Nitrate, Pesticides and Lead – 1989 and 1990*. London: Drinking Water Inspectorate.

Dudley, N., 1986, *Nitrates in Food and Water*. London: London Food Commission.

Dudley, N., 1991, *Good Health on a Polluted Planet*. London: Thorsons.

Elsworth, S., 1990, *A Dictionary of the Environment*. London: Paladin.

Elwood, M., 1989, 'Epidemiology of Melanoma: Its Relationship to Ultraviolet Radiation and Ozone Depletion', in Russell Jones, R., and Wigley, T., (eds), *Ozone Depletion: Health and Environmental Consequences*. London: John Wiley.

Environment Digest, published by Environmental Publications, Cambridge.

European Commission, 1992, *Amended Proposal for a Council Directive on Ozone* (COM(92)236).

European Community, 1976, *Directive concerning the Quality of Bathing Water* (Directive 76/160/EEC).

European Community, 1980a, *Directive relating to the Quality of Water Intended for Human Consumption* (Directive 80/778/EEC).

European Community, 1980b, *Directive on Air Quality Limit Values and Guide Values for Sulphur Dioxide and Suspended Particulates* (Directive 80/779/EEC).

European Community, 1985, *Directive on Air Quality Standards for Nitrogen Dioxide* (Directive 85/203/EEC).

Fenske, R., 1992, 'Differences in Exposure Potential for Adults and Children following Residential Pesticide Applications', in Guzelian, P., Henry, C., and Olin, S., (eds), *Similarities and Differences between Children and Adults: Implications for Risk Assessment*. Washington DC, USA: International Life Sciences Institute.

Flekkøy, M., 1991, *A Voice for Children*. London: Jessica Kingsley Publishers.

Friends of the Earth, 1990, *Cryptosporidium* (unpublished briefing paper).

Friends of the Earth, 1991, *Bathing Water*. London: Friends of the Earth.

Fulton, M., et al, 1987, Influence of blood lead on the ability and attainment of children in Edinburgh, *The Lancet*, 30 May 1987.

Furley, A., 1989, *A Bad Start in Life – Children, Health and Housing*. London: Shelter.

Gallup Political and Economic Index, published by Gallup, London.

Gardner, M., et al, 1990, Results of case-control study of leukaemia and lymphoma among young people near Sellafield nuclear plant in West Cumbria, *British Medical Journal*, 17 February 1990, vol 300, pp 423-9.

Goldsmith, E., and Hildyard, N., 1990, *The Earth Report 2*. London: Mitchell Beazley.

Good Holiday, published by Hill Publications, Epsom, Surrey.

Goren, A., and Hellmann, S., 1988, Prevalence of respiratory symptoms and diseases in schoolchildren living in a polluted and in a low polluted area in Israel, *Environmental Research*, February 1988, vol 45, pp 28-37.

Green, N., 1991, *Poisoning our Children*. Chicago: Noble Press.

Green, P., 1992, Ignoring the risks, *Safe Energy*, February/March 1992.

Greenpeace, 1991a, *The Environmental Impact of the Car*. Amsterdam: Greenpeace International.

Greenpeace, 1991b, *Burning Questions – Incineration in the UK*. London: Greenpeace UK.

Greenpeace, 1992, *Gasping for Change*. London: Greenpeace UK.

Group of Experts on the Scientific Aspects of Marine Pollution, 1990, *The State of the Marine Environment*. Nairobi, Kenya: United Nations Environment Programme.

Haigh, N., 1990, *EEC Environmental Policy and Britain*. Harlow: Longman.

Haines, A., 1990, 'The Implications for Health', in Leggett, J. (ed), *Global Warming*. Oxford: Oxford University Press.

Health and Safety Executive, 1992, *Pesticides Incidents Investigated in 1991/92*. Bootle: HSE.

Her Majesty's Inspectorate of Pollution, 1990, *Second Annual Report* 1988-89. London: HMSO.

Hillman, M., 1991, *Uses and Abuses of Transport and Road Safety Statistics in Policy Formation*. Manchester: Manchester Statistical Society.

Hillman, M., Adams, J., and Whitelegg, J., 1990, *One False Move ... A Study of Children's Independent Mobility*. London: Policy Studies Institute.

Holman, C., and Festing, S., 1991, *Air Quality and Health*. London: Friends of the Earth.

House of Commons Environment Committee, 1990, *Pollution of Beaches*. London: HMSO.

Humber, S., 1992, *Chemical Waste Disposal – The Environmentally Acceptable Alternatives*, speech given at Institute of Corrosion conference, 12/13 May 1992.

Hunter, J., 1986, 'The Distribution of Lead', in Lansdown, R., and Yule, W., (eds), *The Lead Debate: The Environment, Toxicology and Child Health*. London: Croom Helm.

Ibarra, J., 1992, Cats, dogs and young families: do they mix?, *Professional Care of Mother and Child*, April 1992.

Institution of Environmental Health Officers, 1992, *Environmental Health Statistics 1990-91*. London: IEHO.

Jaspert, J., Cavanagh, S., and Debono, J., 1988, *Thinking of Small Children: Access, Provision and Play*. London: We Welcome Small Children Campaign, Women's Design Service and London Borough of Camden.

Koenig, J., et al, Prior exposure to ozone potentiates subsequent response to sulfur dioxide in adolescent asthmatic subjects, *American Review of Respiratory Disease*, February 1990, vol 141, pp 377-380.

Lader, D., and Matheson, J., 1990, *Smoking among Secondary School Children in 1990*. London: HMSO.

Lambert, G., and Hsu, C., 1992, 'Polyhalogenated Biphenyls and the Developing Human', in Guzelian, P., Henry, C., and Olin, S., (eds), *Similarities and Differences between Children and Adults: Implications for Risk Assessment.* Washington DC, USA: International Life Sciences Institute.

Lang, T., and Clutterbuck, C., 1991, *P is for Pesticides.* London: Ebury Press.

Lawson, S., 1990, *Accidents to Young Pedestrians: Distributions, Circumstances, Consequences and Scope for Countermeasures.* Basingstoke: AA Foundation for Road Safety Research.

Leeds University Centre for Clinical Epidemiology, 1990, *Leukaemia and Lymphoma: An Atlas of Distribution within Areas of England and Wales.* London: Leukaemia Research Fund.

Leicester City Council, 1992, *Policy for Street Play: A Child-Friendly Approach to Urban Traffic Management,* committee paper.

Link, A., 1991, *Chlorine, Pollution and the Parents of Tomorrow.* London: Women's Environmental Network.

London Food Commission, 1988, *Food Adulteration and How to Beat It.* London: Unwin.

Love, G., Lan, S., and Shy, C., 1982, Acute respiratory illness in families exposed to nitrogen dioxide ambient air pollution in Chattanooga, Tennessee, *Archives of Environmental Health,* March/April 1982, vol 37, pp 75-80.

McConville, B., 1990, *The Parents' Green Guide.* London: Pandora.

MacKie, R., 1992, *Healthy Skin: The Facts.* Oxford: Oxford University Press.

Mansfield, P., and Monro, J., 1987, *Chemical Children.* London: Century Hutchinson.

Mellanby, K., 1992, *Waste and Pollution.* London: Harper Collins.

Merke, D., and Miller, R., 1992, 'Age Differences in the Effects of Ionizing Radiation', in Guzelian, P., Henry, C., and Olin, S., (eds), *Similarities and Differences between Children and Adults: Implications for Risk Assessment.* Washington DC, USA: International Life Sciences Institute.

Michell, L., 1990, *Growing Up in Smoke.* London: Pluto Press

Ministry of Agriculture, Fisheries and Food, 1989, *Lead in Food:*

Progress Report (Food Surveillance Paper No. 27). London: HMSO.

Moore, M., Meredith, P., and Goldberg, A., 1977, A retrospective analysis of blood-lead in mentally retarded children, *The Lancet*, 2 April 1977.

Mostardi, R., et al, 1981, The University of Akron study of air pollution and human health effects II: Effects on acute respiratory illness, *Archives of Environmental Health*, September/October 1981, vol 36, pp 250-255.

National Association for the Care and Resettlement of Offenders, 1988, *A Review of the Play and Recreational Needs of Young People Growing Up on Housing Estates*. London: NACRO.

National Audit Office, 1991, *Repair and Maintenance of School Buildings*. London: HMSO.

National Radiological Protection Board, 1992, *Electromagnetic Fields and the Risk of Cancer*. Didcot: NRPB.

National Rivers Authority, 1992, *Bathing Water Quality in England and Wales 1991*. Bristol: NRA.

Needleman, H., et al, 1979, Deficits in psychologic and classroom performance of children with elevated dentine lead levels, *New England Journal of Medicine*, vol 300, pp 689-695.

Ninan, T., and Russell, G., 1992, Respiratory symptoms and atopy in Aberdeen schoolchildren: evidence from two surveys 25 years apart, *British Medical Journal*, 4 April 1992, vol 304, pp 873-5.

Parkinson, C., 1987, *Children's Range Behaviour*. Birmingham: Play Board.

Platt, S.D. et al, 1989, Damp housing, mould growth and symptomatic health state, *British Medical Journal*, 24 June 1989, vol 298, pp 1673-8.

Play Board, 1985, *Make Way for Children's Play*. Birmingham: Play Board.

Plunkett, L., Turnbull, D., and Rodricks, J., 1992, 'Differences between Adults and Children Affecting Exposure Assessment', in Guzelian, P., Henry, C., and Olin, S., (eds), *Similarities and Differences between Children and Adults: Implications for Risk*

Assessment. Washington DC, USA: International Life Sciences Institute.

Pönkä, A., 1990, Absenteeism and respiratory disease among children and adults in Helsinki in relation to low-level air pollution and temperature, *Environmental Research,* June 1990, vol 52, pp 34-46.

Potter, S., and Hughes, 1990, *Vital Travel Statistics.* Milton Keynes: Open University.

Preston, B., 1992, *Cutting Pedestrian Casualties.* London: Transport and Health Study Group.

Radford, E., 1987, 'Recent Evidence of Radiation-induced Cancer in the Japanese Atomic Bomb Survivors', in Russell Jones, R., and Southwood. R., (eds), *Radiation and Health.* London: John Wiley.

Read, C., 1991, *Air Pollution and Child Health.* London: Greenpeace UK.

Read, R., and Green, M., 1990, Internal combustion and health, *British Medical Journal,* 24 March 1990, vol 300, pp 761-2.

Roberts, R., 1992, 'Overview of Similarities and Differences between Children and Adults: Implications for Risk Assessment', in Guzelian, P., Henry, C., and Olin, S., (eds), *Similarities and Differences between Children and Adults: Implications for Risk Assessment.* Washington DC, USA: International Life Sciences Institute.

Rose, C., 1990, *The Dirty Man of Europe.* London: Simon & Schuster.

Rosenbaum, M., and Newell, P., 1991, *Taking Children Seriously – A Proposal for a Children's Rights Commissioner.* London: Gulbenkian Foundation.

Royal College of Physicians, 1992, *Smoking and the Young.* London: Royal College of Physicians.

Royal Commission on Environmental Pollution, 1983, *Lead in the Environment.* London: HMSO.

Royal Commission on Environmental Pollution, 1992, *Freshwater Quality.* London: HMSO.

Russell Jones, R., 1989, The continuing hazard of lead in drinking water, *The Lancet*, 16 September 1989.

Rutishauser, M., et al, 1990, Significant association between outdoor NO_2 and respiratory symptoms in preschool children, *Lung*, vol 168 supplement 1990, pp 347-352.

Sabin, A., 1991, letter from Director of Environmental Services, Swale Borough Council, to residents of Church Milton Estate, Sittingbourne, Kent, 26 February 1991.

Simpson, S., 1990, *The Times Guide to the Environment*. London: Times Books.

Spektor, D., at al, 1988, Effects of ambient ozone on respiratory function in active, normal children, *American Review of Respiratory Disease*, February 1988, vol 137, pp 313-320.

Timberlake, L., and Thomas, L., 1990, *When the Bough Breaks*. London: Earthscan.

Townswomen's Guilds, 1991, *Danger – Children at Play*. Birmingham: Townswomen's Guilds.

United Kingdom Co-ordinating Committee on Cancer Research, 1992, *Unique National Survey of Children's Cancer to Begin in April*, press release, 12 March 1992.

United Nations, 1989, *The Convention on the Rights of the Child*. Geneva: Defence for Children International and the United Nations Children's Fund.

United Nations Children's Fund (UNICEF)/United Nations Environment Programme (UNEP), 1990, *Children and the Environment*. New York: UNICEF/UNEP.

Urquhart, J., 1987, *Leukaemia and Nuclear Power in Britain*. London: Friends of the Earth.

Urquhart, J., et al, 1991, Case-control study of leukaemia and non-Hodgkin's lymphoma in children in Caithness near the Dounreay nuclear installation, *British Medical Journal*, 23 March 1991, vol 302, no 6778, pp 687-691.

Walters, S., Griffiths, R., and Ayres, J., 1992, *Spatial Distribution of Hospital Admissions for Asthma and Their Relationship to Ambient Air Pollution Levels*. Birmingham: University of Birmingham Institute of Public and Environmental Health.

Ward, C., 1978, *The Child in the City*. London: Architectural Press.

Ward, C., 1988, *The Child in the Country*. London: Bedford Square Press.

Ware, C., et al, 1986, Effects of ambient sulfur oxides and suspended particulates on respiratory health of preadolescent children, *American Review of Respiratory Disease*, May 1986, vol 133, pp 834-842.

Warren Spring Laboratory, 1992, *Initial Analysis of NO_2 Pollution Episode, December 1991*. Stevenage: Warren Spring Laboratory.

Water Research Centre, 1992, *Economics of Lead Pipe Replacement* (unpublished).

Water Supply (Water Quality) Regulations 1989 (SI 1989/1147). London: HMSO.

Wertheimer, N., and Leeper, E., 1979, Electrical wiring configurations and childhood cancer, *American Journal of Epidemiology*, vol 109, p273.

Which?, published by the Consumers' Association, London.

Whitehead, M., 1988, *The Health Divide*. London: Penguin.

Wilson, D., 1983, *The Lead Scandal*. London: Heinemann.

Women's Design Service, 1992, *Factsheet 1: Access, Factsheet 2: Babycare*, and *Factsheet 3: Play*. London: Women's Design Service.

World Health Organisation, 1986, *Principles for Evaluating Health Risks from Chemicals during Infancy and Early Childhood*. Geneva: WHO.

Index

Humber, S, 41
Humberside, 67
Hunter, J, 10
hydrocarbons, 22, 26, 30, 33

I
Ibarra, J, 42
ICI, 30
IKEA, 66
Ilford, 41
immune system, 4, 28, 35, 37
incineration, 28, 31, 34
Independent, The, 21, 28, 32, 59, 73, 76
indoor pollution, 4, 50, 53, 71-73, 78
industrial pollution, 5, 6, 19, 22, 24, 27, 28, 30, 31, 36, 38, 39, 41, 47, 76
inland waters, 44-45
Institution of Environmental Health Officers, 11, 51
International Commission on Radiological Protection, 50
iodine, 50
Israel, 25

J
Jaspert, J, 65

K
Kent, 41
Koenig, J, 29

L
Lader, D, 71, 72
Lambert, G, 28
Lan, S, 21
Lancaster University, 43
landfill, 16, 40
Lang, T, 42
Lawson, S, 58
lead, 5, 19, 41
  in air, 8, 26-27
  in drinking water, 8-12, 16, 76, 78, 79
  in dust, 27
  in food, 27
  in petrol, 8, 10, 26-27, 79

lead-free petrol, 27
Leeds University, 51
Leeper, E, 52
Leicester City Council, 69
Leigh Environmental, 31
length of journeys, 55
leptospirosis, 45
leukaemia, 27, 47-50, 51, 52
lime, 12
Link, A, 29
Llandudno, 42
local authorities, 11, 17, 19, 33, 34, 39, 41, 45, 51, 53, 63, 68-69, 70, 74, 76, 77
London, 18, 21, 24, 25, 26, 30, 41, 53, 68, 73
London Docklands Development Corporation, 30
London Food Commission, 13, 14
Los Angeles, 30
Lothian, 71, 72
Love Canal, 40
Love, G, 21
Lullington Heath, Sussex, 22
Lyme Regis, 42

M
M25 motorway, 32
MacKie, R, 35
Manchester, 21, 68
Mansfield, 24
Mansfield, P, 13
Marks & Spencer, 65
Marshall Islands, 48
Matheson, J, 71, 72
McConville, B, 14
Medical Research Council, 19, 32
Mellanby, K, 24
Meredith, P, 9
Merke, D, 48
Merseyside, 10
methaemoglobinaemia, 13
methane, 38
methyl chloroform, 36
Michell, L, 71, 72
microwaves, 52
Midlands, 10, 13
Miller, R, 48

radiotherapy, 47
radon, 46, 50-51, 53, 71
rail travel, 54, 61-62, 65
rats, 45
Read, C, 23, 24, 25, 28, 32
Read, R, 26
ReChem, 31
respiratory problems, 4, 5, 19-26,
    29-32, 42, 72-73, 78
Rhyl, 42
Ripon, Yorkshire, 14
rivers: see inland waters
road traffic
    accidents, 6, 56-59, 79
    air pollution, 5, 18, 19, 20, 22, 23,
        25, 26, 27, 28, 30, 31, 32, 33,
        34, 38, 54, 78, 79
    forecasts, 33
    impact on children's independent
        freedom of movement, 6, 59-61,
        63, 66, 79
    play streets and child pedestrian
        priority, 69
    traffic calming, 59, 63, 79
road-building, 34
Roberts, R, 20
Rodricks, J, 3, 4, 7, 19
Rose, C, 11, 44
Rosenbaum, M, 80
Rotterdam, 67
Royal College of Physicians, 49, 72
Royal Commission on Environmental
    Pollution, 12, 45
rural areas, 22, 67, 68
Russell Jones, R, 10
Russell, G, 32
Rutishauser, M, 22

S
Sabin, A, 41
Safeway, 65
Sainsbury's, 65
salmonella, 43
schools, 10, 16, 25, 37, 39, 41, 52,
    59, 63, 65, 73, 75-76, 77
Scotland, 10, 11, 12, 42, 49, 50, 71, 72
Scottish Office, 57
Sellafield, 48-49, 51

Sheffield, 15, 21, 31
Shy, C, 21
simazine, 15
Simpson, S, 24, 47
skin cancer, 35, 36-37
Smith, S, 7
smog, 18, 21, 25, 29-30, 79
smoke, 18-19, 24, 25-26, 29-30
social class, 6, 57
Solent, 44
Solicitors Journal, 31
Somerset, 49, 51
South West England, 10
Southampton, 31
Southampton University, 49
Southend, 44
Southern England, 42
Southport, 42
Spektor, D, 23
spray drift, 42, 45
Stockholm, 62
Stockport, 67
sulphur dioxide, 19, 23-25, 26, 29,
    31, 32
Sunday Times, 30
supermarkets, 65
Surrey, 15
Sweden, 62, 67, 80
Swindon, 15
Switzerland, 21

T
Tesco, 65
Thames Water, 14
Thomas, L, 2, 13, 29, 38
Timberlake, L, 2, 13, 29, 38
time values, 56
Times, The, 28
tower blocks, 74
Townswomen's Guilds, 67
toxocariasis, 41-42
traffic: see road traffic
trihalomethanes, 15
Turnbull, D, 3, 4, 7, 19

U
UK Co-ordinating Committee on
    Cancer Research, 52

98